70 Years of God's Miracles

Basil "Buzz" Howell

TRILOGY CHRISTIAN PUBLISHERS
TUSTIN, CA

Trilogy Christian Publishers
A Wholly Owned Subsidiary of Trinity Broadcasting Network
2442 Michelle Drive
Tustin, CA 92780

For information, address Trilogy Christian Publishing

Rights Department, 2442 Michelle Drive, Tustin, Ca 92780.

Trilogy Christian Publishing/ TBN and colophon are trademarks of Trinity Broadcasting Network.

For information about special discounts for bulk purchases, please contact Trilogy Christian Publishing.

Manufactured in the United States of America

Trilogy Disclaimer: The views and content expressed in this book are those of the author and may not necessarily reflect the views and doctrine of Trilogy Christian Publishing or the Trinity Broadcasting Network.

10 9 8 7 6 5 4 3 2 1

Library of Congress Cataloging-in-Publication Data is available.

ISBN 978-1-63769-252-3

ISBN 978-1-63769-253-0(ebook)

Acknowledgements

There are numerous people who helped make this book possible, starting with my lovely wife, Esperanza, the love of my life. Her imprint is all over this memoir about our life together. I also want to thank our four children, eight grandchildren, and four great-grandchildren who have been a loving, godly blessing throughout our lives and offer a significant future for years to come—a special shout out to Chezaraye and Gavin for all their data entry.

I also want to acknowledge my younger brother, Wade, for sharing some of his experiences from our younger years. Plus, daughter Charlene and husband Frank for helping me tremendously by recalling times, dates, and sometimes what really happened. A fantastic thank- you to everyone who wrote sidebars sharing their thoughts, memories, and love. We will treasure them forever.

In addition, I want to thank Ken Walker, my co-author and editor, who was a true motivation to me in many ways.

A final word of thanks to the numerous mentors and pastors who have enriched my life in business and spiritually. They include:

- Business training: Dr. Ross Atkinson, head of the business department, San Jose (California) City College, 1962–1963.
- Automotive career: While there were several, two who stand out are Bob Rausch, used car manager of All American Pontiac-GMC, 1969–1970, and general manager of Autocar Europe-Volvo, 1971–1972; also Don Lucas, owner of Autocar Europe and Don Lucas Cadillac, 1971–1979.

There have been many Christian leaders and pastors who have blessed my life—more than I can list here. A special mention to:

- Bob Rausch, who didn't just work with me in the car business but was a great friend for many years.
- Rich Marshall, pastor of Crossroads Church in San Jose, California.
- Jim Woodall, pastor of our home ministry in Los Gatos, California, who now lives in Pueblo, Colorado, and has had a ministry in Nicaragua for more than thirty years.

- Kenny Foreman, pastor of Cathedral of Faith in San Jose, California.
- Herb Valero, pastor of Victory Outreach in Salinas, California.
- Greg Massanari, pastor of Cornerstone Church, Las Vegas.
- Drew Moore, pastor of Canyon Ridge Church, Las Vegas.

Contents

Foreword

There is more in this book than you might expect. On the surface, it may appear to be the wonderful—even miraculous—story of one man's life. But while that should be enough, there is much, much more.

My wife, Wilma, and I had the privilege to be a part of the story within these pages as pastors of the church Buzz and Espe Howell attended during the early stages of their walk with Christ. Those truly were some "good old days," and we have fond memories of seeing God at work in our midst, things like a growing church, hundreds of refugees from Southeast Asia experiencing the wonder of God's grace, and a new awareness of God's power. In short, almost everything we should expect to see in a vibrant, local church ministry.

Yet, God was doing something far bigger than our congregation, even bigger than Buzz and Espe knew. In this book, you will read of his powerful conversion in a confessional with a Catholic priest. You will also read of how friends from the automobile business, Bob and Karen Rausch, brought them to Crossroads Bible Church in San Jose, California, where I was then pastor.

Although we did not recognize it at the time, those two seemingly unrelated events were signs of God bringing forth two globally significant, world-shaping movements. What historians now recognize as the charismatic renewal (including the charismatic Catholic renewal) and the Marketplace Ministry movement was being birthed right before our eyes. It would be years before Wilma and I personally experienced the wonderful, miraculous power of the Holy Spirit. We knew Him and believed in Him, but it wasn't until a meeting in an upper room of a restaurant in Argentina that we were fully and powerfully "filled with the Spirit." And it would be years later before God began using us to minister in the marketplace.

As you read the story of Buzz Howell's stirring experiences with God, you will see the convergence of these two world-shaking movements. Though we were part of it, it was all so new to us and so early in their development that we almost missed it. As I write these words, I rejoice that we didn't and that we remained open and seeking for the "more" that God has for us. Not only did we find it—today, we are still discovering it.

So, I encourage you to read this book and rejoice in what God has done with and through one of His "unknown soldiers"! But don't stop there; look for the plan

God has for you. Read with a sense of expectancy and anticipation for the miracles you will see, for the lives that you will touch, and for the unexpected and perfect plan God has for you.

Thank you, Buzz and Espe Howell! Your faith has touched many! And now, with a faith-filled look at the future, we cry out, "More, Lord, for Your glory."

—Rich Marshall
Castle Rock, Colorado
Author: *God@Work* (Volumes 1 & 2)
Host: God@Work on GodTV

CHAPTER 1

Verification of Heaven

Then I looked, and I heard the voice of many angels around the throne, the living creatures, and the elders; and the number of them was ten thousand times ten thousand, and thousands of thousands, saying with a loud voice: "Worthy is the Lamb who was slain to receive power and riches and wisdom, and strength and honor and glory and blessing!"
Revelation 5:11-12

Heaven. There is simply nothing like it on the human plane of existence. It is dazzling in its perfection, with its brilliance unfolding with more majesty than a thousand peacocks. Color of a multitude of shades of familiar hues, and others not seen on our planet, exist in heaven. They shine in such a way the best comparison I can make is of a rainbow composed of hundreds of rainbows. This nearly indescribable palate covered every inch of heaven. Even if all I saw the day I went to heaven were its cornucopia of colors, I would sing its praises—and the God who reigns over it—for the rest of my days.

Yet there was more. So much more.

Music that pulsated with intensity, and yet soothed with perfect harmonies, wafted over me. As it reverberated in my spirit, I felt sensations and thrills rising within; I now knew what pure music felt like. Choirs stretching beyond the horizon sang in voices that can best be described as angelic. I joined in the melodious praise and worship, able to understand every song even if I had never heard it before. Joy flooded my spirit as I reveled in a newfound awareness and sensitivity to everything around me. I could feel the love of God filling every fiber of my being.

Another thing that impressed me was the calm in the atmosphere. No one rushed around or looked over their shoulder with anxiety etched into their countenance. No one checked their watches, scanned their to-do lists, fretted about the bills, worried about tomorrow, or fought for a place at the head of the line. It was beyond wonderful. Imagine taking a vacation to a picturesque, luxurious Hawaiian island with the weather so balmy you never need a jacket. And while you're there, you stay in a windowless villa, dining whenever you chose from an endless buffet, as a retinue of servants waits on you hand and foot.

Heaven is a hundred times better.

Unexpected Trip

Then I turned to see the voice that spoke with me. And having turned I saw seven golden lampstands, and in the midst of the seven lampstands One like the Son of Man, clothed with a garment down to the feet and girded about the chest with a golden band. His head and hair were white like wool, as white as snow, and His eyes like a flame of fire; His feet were like fine brass, as if refined in a furnace, and His voice as the sound of many waters; He had in His right hand seven stars, out of His mouth went a sharp two-edged sword, and His countenance was like the sun shining in its strength.

Revelation 1:12-16

My trip began with an unexpected interruption in the midst of a sunny July day in 1984 in Northern California. My beautiful wife, Esperanza—which means "hope" in English—and I went out for breakfast near our home in Los Gatos prior to heading to San Jose's Spartan Stadium (since renamed CEFCU Stadium for Citizens Equity First Credit Union) to watch the Golden

Bay Earthquakes play soccer. Near the end of the game, though, sudden pains shot through my stomach. They increased with such intensity that I thought I would pass out.

After considerable groaning and slumping over in my seat, Espe rushed me out the gate and into our car before heading pell-mell down the highway to a hospital close to our home. When we arrived, my wife's shouts brought some nurses running. After hooking me up to equipment and taking my vital signs, one told her, "your husband's appendix is about to burst."

Shock washing over her, Espe struggled to grasp the significance of what she had just learned. She didn't want to believe it! When she regained her senses, she immediately began praying for my well-being and a safe surgery. God responded by giving her the kind of peace that passes all understanding. She knew her prayers would be answered.

I wish I could say I felt the same way. As a couple of aides wheeled me to an emergency operating room, I struggled with fear and the worst case of nerves I have ever known. Like my wife, though, after regaining my senses, I prayed and asked God for His help. I asked that He guide the surgeon's hands and that the operation would be successful.

No sooner had they administered the medication to put me asleep than I felt myself lifting up, up, and up out of the operating room. Unable to believe my eyes at first, I found myself in heaven. How did I know this? I just knew. For one, I felt complete peace of mind, tranquility, and a deep sense of belonging. It was unlike any place I had ever visited. I felt totally at home with being there, like one of countless kindred spirits. Joy and happiness overwhelmed me.

As I looked across a vast expanse of sky, my eyes widened. There were so many things to see all at once and so much happening. While on an earthly plane, there would be no way to absorb everything that was going on; in heaven, it all felt normal. I felt very much at home. There was no worry, no fear, and no reason to get upset. I knew that everything was in God's hands and within His control. As I floated above millions of people, I heard them praising God in their native languages. Though I struggle to speak anything but English, I understood all their words! In fact, I joined in the praise with my own heavenly language. When I noticed they all were raising their hands, I raised mine too as we worshiped God Almighty.

A Place for Us

> *In My Father's house are many mansions; if it were not so, I would have told you. I go to prepare a place for you. And if I go and prepare a place for*

you, I will come again and receive you to Myself;
that where I am, there you may be also.

John 14:2-3

By now, you may be wondering: "So what's so great about this guy's experience? Haven't we already had a flood of books about the beyond? Hasn't 90 Minutes in Heaven sold a truckload of copies? Even been made into a movie?" While I would answer "yes" to all those questions, I still feel compelled by the Lord to share what happened to me. Not just because I saw and felt such an awe-inspiring vision as I lay on the operating table. Besides that, my entire life has been an affirmation of the God who didn't just create me but saved me—more than once—years before this experience. This is a memoir about Him and the incredible miracles I have seen Him perform throughout my more than seven decades on this earth.

I am starting with my trip to heaven because it is such a stirring, almost unbelievable story. Were it not for living through it, I would be as skeptical as some of you reading these words. I might be wondering if you had made it all up, eaten too much pizza the night before, or had strange hallucinations while on anesthesia. I assure you: it was real. Every time I think about it or my wife brings it up, I go back in time, and a smile crosses my face—feelings of joy dance through my heart and spirit.

We have to understand God created this earth and prepared a place to spend eternity for those who truly believe in Him, as Jesus assured His disciples in John 14:2-3. For some reason, which I assume will be revealed to me when I enter heaven for the last time, God blessed me with this preview of my final resting place. I have led a fairly long life, one that has included some pretty tough years, as well as rewarding times. Yet nothing that takes place on this planet can match the grandeur of heaven.

Heaven is where everyone wants to go at the end of life (especially when the other choice is hell). It offers perfect peace, tranquility, and the sense of belonging and community that so many spend years of their existence desperately hoping to discover. In heaven, I felt love emanating from God that was far superior to any earthly kind.

Entering the Throne Room

Immediately I was in the Spirit; and behold, a throne set in heaven, and One sat on the throne. And He who sat there was like a jasper and a sardius stone in appearance; and there was a rainbow around the throne, in appearance like an emerald. Around the throne were twenty-four thrones, and on the thrones I saw twenty-four elders sitting, clothed in white robes; and they had crowns of gold on their heads.

Revelation 4:2-4

Everything in heaven was so natural, including the lighting, that it felt like living through a cinematic experience. It was more lifelike than any IMAX theater or Dolby Atmos surround-sound system. Earlier I mentioned the breathtaking rainbows in heaven. Not surprisingly, since God gave Noah the rainbow a sign of His covenant to never again destroy the earth with a flood (Genesis 9:13-16), they occupy a dominant place in heaven. That includes God's throne room, a place so magnificent that words can't fully capture its full dimensions. It is filled with majesty, royalty, and beauty—a true feast for the eyes.

As I reached the throne room, I tried to imagine who could be there. I could envision Old Testament leaders and prophets like Moses, Abraham, Joseph, Joshua, Noah, David, Solomon, and Daniel. And such New Testament figures as Paul, Peter, James, and Gospel writers Matthew, Mark, Luke, and John. And, of course, Jesus the Christ, our Savior.

Ironically, the solid glass enclosure and the brightness and a dazzling rainbow of colors made it difficult to discern exactly who was there. Yet through the wide opening, I could see there were people walking around. That I couldn't identify them didn't upset me. I knew heaven was where I belonged. I was a part of everything happening in heaven. Because of that trip, Colossians 3:1 has become one of my favorite Scriptures: "If you then were raised with Christ, desire those things which are above, where Christ sits at the right hand of God" (MEV).

These words have fascinating meaning to me for several reasons:

1. I rose up to heaven.
2. Things on earth are no longer that meaningful by comparison.
3. The only disappointment I experienced afterward was coming back to earth.

The heavenly music was so intense it sounded like an orchestra of millions were playing in perfect tune, accompanied by a similar-size choir singing every song to perfection. As a boy, I liked lavish movie musicals with big orchestras, great singing, and fantastic ending numbers. No matter how much money is spent, what famed composers write the music, or what stars they employ, no Hollywood production could ever hope to match the music in heaven.

Equally amazing is how I was able to absorb all the sight sounds. I was prepared for anything God allowed me to see, feel, or be a part of there. My senses were heightened at a level unheard of this world, all rolled up into a ball of happiness and natural joy. While the music pulsated throughout my being, I followed everything with my eyes and could understand everything without any struggle. I sang and worshiped in tune and knew all the words, so I never distracted the worship. While that may not sound that impressive, you need to appreciate that in real life, I cannot hold a note with both hands.

Affirming the Vision

> Whenever the living creatures give glory and honor and thanks to Him who sits on the throne, who lives forever and ever, the twenty-four elders fall down before Him who sits on the throne and worship Him who lives forever and ever, and cast their crowns before the throne, saying: "You are worthy, O Lord, to receive glory and honor and power; for You created all things, and by Your will they exist and were created."
>
> Revelation 4:9-11

I went to heaven about five years before Don Piper's visit in January of 1989. He later wrote *90 Minutes in Heaven* (and several succeeding titles) with prolific ghostwriter and author Cecil Murphey. Although Baker Publishing's Revell imprint only released 7,500 copies initially, since then, it has sold more than five million. I am a huge fan of the book and used to buy them in lots of ten to hand out to nonbelievers.

One reason I absorbed the book so intently was that I could relate to a succession of Piper's experiences. Having lived through what I did, his book had the ring of authenticity. For example, in chapter two, he writes of how time had no meaning. Bingo! There are no clocks in heaven, no rush to get across town or pick up your kids or make it to a doctor's appointment or any of a dozen different reasons we dash around like the proverbial chicken without a head. Just total peace and harmony, all under God's control.

Like Piper, I have to use earthly terms to describe the unimaginable excitement, warmth, and happiness in heaven, but they pale by comparison to the real thing. As Paul wrote in the apocryphal "love chapter," 1 Corinthians 13: "For now we see in a mirror, dimly, but then face to face. Now I know in part, but then I shall know just as I also am known" (v. 12). When it comes to heaven, we can only see in a dim mirror what awaits us. If more people fully grasped the awesomeness of what awaits everyone who follows Jesus as Lord, the lines of those seeking to enter heaven would stretch around the globe.

Piper also writes about a first-class buffet for the senses. I know exactly how that feels. Even though I found myself floating above millions of people, my senses and eyes could absorb everything with fantastic visual intake. It felt like I was zeroing in with crystal clear vision of a melodious opera singer while admiring from the back row of the balcony. It wasn't just my keen eyesight. I found myself with an extraordinary ability to smell, hear, perceive, and experience everything around me. It left me with a lasting catalog of memories.

With all five senses dramatically multiplied, I could see the brilliant light and rainbows emanating from God's throne room as I drew closer to it. I believe its brightness was the reason I couldn't determine who was present. I know it all sounds unbelievable, but how can one adequately explain living in another dimension? It is strange being in the hospital for surgery and an instant later being in heaven. But it was...well, heavenly. Piper talks about every feature being perfect and beautiful—wonderful to gaze at. As he writes: "Everything was perfect. I sensed that I knew everything and had no questions to ask."[1]

Indeed, everything had an order and structure to it like nothing we can see on earth. This is one of the most difficult things to explain; when people hear my descriptions, many scoff, "no one and nothing is perfect." All I can say in response is: "God is perfect, so He created a perfect heaven." How else can I explain being able to sing in perfect voice and rhythm when down here I sound like a screech owl whose feathers are getting plucked? How could I have been part of something greater than anyone can explain?

Being magnificent in love, worship, and praise is not bragging about my abilities but the God who made it possible. It was an overflowing feast for my ears. I didn't make a decision to follow Christ until my late thirties. Yet, after only four years of walking with Christ, I was participating in the greatest concert of all time. If it sounds unbelievable to you, imagine how I felt! It's nearly impossible to explain in the natural, but heaven is where God allows His children to experience the supernatural organized by our divine Creator. Everything in heaven is perfect, even a thousand songs playing simultaneously. Imagine the cacophony of discordant sounds if you tried that on earth.

Longing for Home

For I am persuaded that neither death nor life, nor angels nor principalities nor powers, nor things present nor things to come, nor height nor depth, nor any other created thing, shall be able to separate us from the love of God which is in Christ Jesus our Lord.

Romans 8:38-39

In the tenth anniversary edition of 90 *Minutes in Heaven*, Piper wrote a personal update about the millions of miles he had traveled, people he had met, and the countless prayers he had seen answered since the book's original release in 2004.

A paragraph near the end of this section particularly stood out to me: "And finally, I stood there at the gates of heaven, more alive and complete than I have ever been here on earth. I was surrounded by those who had preceded me in death and who helped me get to heaven by their words and actions. This remains the most real experience of my entire existence. Though I chose to keep it a sacred secret for a while, I now happily and without reservation shout, 'Heaven is real and Jesus is the Way!'"[2]

I know just how he feels. Although it has been more than thirty-five years since my trip to heaven, my mind thinks of it as clearly as if it happened yesterday. I have cherished it ever since and can hardly wait to go back. Among the many things I anticipate is being able to determine exactly who was walking around in God's throne room. That day in 1984, I was home. Just as Piper says, I wanted to be there more than anywhere else I had ever been on earth. It is where my spirit belongs.

Whenever the subject of heaven comes up in conversation, what immediately comes to mind is *perfection*. Invariably, my mind goes back to that day in the hospital, and all the joy rushes back as I focus my thoughts on the experience. One reason I am convinced of the reality of this is what my wife told me later, about how I had gone through surgery with my arms locked straight up, pointing to heaven. The nurse tried several times to lower my arms, but she couldn't budge them. Finally, she asked the doctor what to do, and he replied, "I'm operating down here. Forget about the arms."

Everyone has a fear of dying, as I once did, but after seeing heaven, I look forward to the day of my return. I truly thank God for what He showed me. Indeed, I long for my return to where my spirit belongs. My human body is getting weaker and slowing down, but I know heaven is my final resting home.

Not everyone can understand this kind of longing. When I awoke after my operation and expressed my overwhelming desire to be back in heaven, Esperanza responded with hurt in her voice, "well, thank you very much." It took a while to fully explain what I had seen, heard, and sensed before she developed the same kind of excitement about her future trip to heaven. If you knew what awaits everyone who professes the name of Jesus as Savior and Lord, you would too!

CHAPTER 2

The Bad Good Old Days

"Wine is a mocker, strong drink is a brawler, and whoever is led astray by it is not wise."

Proverbs 20:1

Do not look on the wine when it is red, when it sparkles in the cup, when it swirls around smoothly; at the last it bites like a serpent, and stings like a viper. Your eyes will see strange things, and your heart will utter perverse things.

Proverbs 23:31-33

Had God not intervened supernaturally thirty-four years earlier, I would have never lived to experience that awe-inspiring visit to heaven. My memories of the incident that nearly claimed my life at age seven are vague. They were likely blocked from my mind by the same God I expect to see on my return trip to heaven.

What I know about the trauma that left emotional and physical scars comes from somewhat-limited accounts from my mother and a younger brother.

To this day, I don't know what demons drove Basil Howell Sr. Maybe it was a painful episode from childhood that flowered into alcohol abuse as he got older. I can imagine that alcohol-fueled episodes were part of his naval service in World War II, which added to the problem. He likely struggled to cope with the pressures of postwar life, too, when he found himself with two children and a wife to support. Ironically, he could have had a great career in sales; in his short stint in the appliance section of a downtown department store in San Jose, California, he was one of the leading salesmen.

Whatever was responsible, a marriage that started out with such love and promise degenerated into an all-out war, sparked by my father's uncontrolled drinking and the unpredictable rages that followed. Sadly, my father never learned the wisdom of Proverbs.

Marriage Match

Susie and Stephen Cunningham, grandparents
Married June 2, 1901, Rulo, Nebraska

My mother, Alyce, was the daughter of Stephen Cunningham, who had moved to Rulo, Nebraska, with his parents from Pennsylvania. My mother's mother was Susie Plante, a native of Quebec, Ontario in Canada, whose family later also settled in Rulo. The Cunningham family's farm had quite a history, dating back to 1844, or thirteen years before the formation of Rulo, a farming town tucked in a corner of southeastern Nebraska. My mother's uncle Benjamin, aunt Mary, and their daughter, Alice, later moved to California to retire at a home located on 4th Street in San Jose, California.

After high school, my mother enrolled at the University of Missouri, where she earned a Bachelor of Science in Journalism in 1938.

Alyce Irene Cunningham

After working for a newspaper in central Missouri, she found a better-paying job with Olan Mills, a national chain of photo studios that was quite popular until falling on hard times in the digital photo age. In her new position, mom traveled throughout the Midwest. While on the road, she met a fellow employee, Basil Auvil Howell.

Considering the tight economic conditions the year they met (1939), my parents were both fortunate to even have landed a job. Olan Mills has a remarkable success story, especially since it launched during the early years of the Depression. Ironically, like my mother's family, founder Olan Mills Sr. was born into a large Nebraska farm family. At the age of twenty-six, he married Mary Stephenson, who had studied art in college. Then living in Selma, Alabama, the newlyweds initially tried their hands at a photograph-copying business. After it went bankrupt, they acquired a studio in Tuscaloosa and eventually went into the portrait business that became their mainstay.

I have always been fascinated with how our lives intersect with so many others. Had there not been an Olan Mills Studio, my parents might have never met. Nor would their jobs have carried them through their first year of marriage. Olan and Mary's business not only made it through the Depression, but it also thrived, especially after Mary created a distinctive style of duotone portraits. Lightly touched up with oil paints, these photos replaced their standard eight-by-ten-inch, black and white prints.

Faster to produce, these new portraits proved quite popular. Olan Mills hired its first traveling photographers in 1935. By 1940, the company had 650 employees turning out twelve thousand portraits a day.

Now, although I know a lot about my mother, the family archives regarding my father are pretty sparse. I don't know his parents' names; my only information

THE BAD GOOD OLD DAYS

comes from an ancestry search a friend did around 2014. Basil Sr. was born on April 18, 1914, in a small mountain town in the central part of West Virginia.

After he and my mother divorced, he wound up in Chicago because no one back home wanted anything to do with him. A sister who corresponded a lot with mom was the only one who would even write him a letter. In true West Virginia fashion, after Basil Sr. died at the VA hospital in Chicago, his family accepted his body for burial close to his hometown.

Change of Scenery

Basil Sr. grew up near Elkins, where he and my mother married on June 24, 1940. Located on the edge of the Monongahela National Forest, Elkins is home to the West Virginia Railroad Museum and is a popular tourist destination. The year after their wedding, they left behind Olan Mills' nomadic lifestyle to open a restaurant in Elkins. Mom worked as a waitress, and dad was the cook, emerging occasionally from the back to chat with customers. In a sad development that foreshadowed the future, as the restaurant prospered, my father started drinking more, which became a source of marital conflict.

Whether the restaurant would have lasted is unknown since World War II intervened at the end of 1941. The day after the Japanese bombed Pearl Harbor on December 7, Congress declared war. In those days, you either enlisted in the military or were drafted, so my father volunteered. Despite his drinking problems, he had taken drafting classes in high school and displayed such aptitude the US Navy gave him a classification of E-5 upon enlistment. That's a mid-level rank that took me several years to attain in the National Guard.

Dad's departure for basic training prompted my mother to return to the familiar climes of Nebraska. Originally, she moved to Rulo to stay with her mother and two sisters. However, my constant crying as a newborn drove her older sister crazy and was the source of numerous arguments. Finally, mom moved about ten miles down the road to an apartment building in Falls City.

My father enlisted in the Seabees, a naval unit formed as a construction battalion, initially for the Pacific Islands. Concerned that war was imminent, in 1940, the navy had initiated a program to erect bases in the Pacific, using civilian contractors. However, after the bombing of Pearl Harbor and the declaration of war that followed, it had to stop using civilian labor.

The Seabees were a marvel of engineering, deployment, and planning, building more than four hundred advanced bases at the cost of nearly eleven billion dollars. These men weren't raw recruits, either. The navy emphasized experience and skill in construction so the workers could adapt civilian experience for military needs. The navy also relaxed traditional physical standards to obtain the necessary personnel.

The typical age for enlistment ranged from eighteen to fifty. But after President Franklin D. Roosevelt (or as he's often known, FDR) halted voluntary enlistments at the end of 1942, the navy had to obtain Seabees through the Selective Service System. Naturally, the average age dropped.

However, during the early days of the war, the average Seabee was thirty-seven years old—or about a decade older than my father. As if he didn't have a bad enough problem with drinking, it's easy to imagine these worldly-wise combat veterans rubbing off on my father in an unhealthy way.

Had he not succumbed to the lures of alcohol, my father could have put his Seabee service to productive use. After all, they were crack units. After the Americans took over an island, the Seabees would build road systems, Quonset encampments, tank farms, supply storage depots, hospitals, ports, harbor facilities, bomber bases, fighter bases, and seaplane bases.

Lean Years

Conceived before dad went off to war, I was born on August 11, 1942. I have no memory of my infant years, but they were lean ones, as the nation struggled to recover from the Great Depression. The October 1929 stock market crash sent the United States into an economic tailspin in the thirties. The "Roaring '20s" that preceded it created such optimism, unrestrained behavior, and foolish speculation that it was only natural for this house of cards to collapse.

FDR did his best to turn things around and create more of a social safety net to help a nation where up to 25 percent of the people were out of work. Yet, by 1939, six years after Roosevelt introduced his New Deal in an effort to relieve our staggering financial problems, unemployment still stood at 17 percent. Nearly a third of the country lived in poverty.

Once World War II began, the nation faced serious restrictions. Kids who today can't imagine being without a Play Station or their smartphone would have trouble wrapping their heads around the idea of everything being rationed, from sugar, coffee, and meat to lard and fruit. At one point, the government enacted a national speed limit of thirty-five miles per hour to save fuel and rubber for tires.

Such circumstances help draw a picture of the burdens ordinary housewives and mothers faced during the war. Mom had finally adjusted to the challenges of being away from my father and her extended family when dad showed up unannounced in the fall of 1943, telling her he had a thirty-day leave. Sixty days later, he hadn't left. Finally, she asked, "aren't you going back?" That's when my father admitted he had deserted. He didn't want to return, but mom blew her stack after learning he was AWOL and declared, "You're going back."

Soon after, she drove him to the naval recruiting office in Falls City to turn himself in. The military never takes unexcused absences lightly. In dad's case, they busted him down from E-5 to E-3 and from draftsman to cook while sending him to the Aleutian Islands. Just off the coast of Alaska, they were the scene of heavy fighting because of their strategic location along the path from Japan.

One other result came from my father's temporary stay in the States: my brother, William. Billy was born on May 25, 1944. And despite his military demotion and punishment, my father made it through the war with no more serious problems. The year after it ended in 1945, we left Nebraska for California to meet my dad. His ship was sailing into Oakland, where he would get his final military discharge papers.

Mom was delighted when she heard this news and purchased train tickets for the long trip west. She had a bit of scare-changing trains in Denver when I walked away from her and got lost in the mammoth crowd at Union Station. Fortunately, an hour later, a policeman found me. As my mom later recalled the story, she was frantic at first and then incredibly relieved when the officer located me.

Alyce, Basil Sr., Billy, Basil Jr.

Struggle for Survival

My mother's aunt Alice had inherited the home at 237 North 4th Street in San Jose after Alice's parents died. Once on her own with such spacious quarters, she turned it into an old-fashioned rooming house, renting out rooms to several other parties. With aunt Alice living so close to Oakland, we naturally gravitated in that direction. Initially, we moved into a suburban, postwar housing development in Mountain View known as

Airport Village. Before long, we packed up and headed for a farmhouse in Santa Clara. During that time, my brother Wade Lynn, who we called Lynnie, was born on February 18, 1947. The following year we moved again into aunt Alice's (I think mom got a break on the rent). Though we never talked about it, I assume the reason for two moves in three years had to do with my parents' strained finances. In some ways, the "good old days" weren't all that good.

Still, I quickly adapted to life in our new surroundings and enrolled at nearby Horace Mann Elementary. Dad started working for Hart's Department Store in downtown San Jose and became one of their best appliance salesmen. Meanwhile, mom helped aunt Alice by collecting rent from two card players living next to us on the first floor, an elderly couple who lived upstairs, and a woman upstairs who worked at the Levi Strauss Factory. She had a son a year younger than me.

Ironically, though I bore my father's name, I looked more like my mother, who had sparkling hazel eyes. My brother, Billy, had dad's blue eyes. While to this day, I'm not sure if dad favored Billy over me, I know he got angry whenever I stepped in to defend mom. In a drunken state, he often took out his frustrations on our mother and would slap her around or hit her. As the oldest boy, I often intervened and took many a beating as my reward.

I assume his drinking is why my father lost his department store job despite a great sales record. With each successive firing, his drinking got worse. Although she tolerated being treated like a punching bag, my mother reached the end of her rope in early 1950, after my drunk-out-of-his-mind father started hollering at me before grabbing my neck. He pressed hard for a few minutes, with the pain intensifying until I finally blacked out.

Naturally, I have no recollection of what happened. But my mother later told me that when she saw me lying there, she started screaming at the top of her lungs, "He killed Bas! He killed Bas! Oh my God!"

She yelled so loudly our neighbors came running. Pouring some water on my face and jostling me, they succeeded in reviving me. An ambulance crew showed up soon after and took me to the hospital.

Fortunately, seven-year-olds are fairly resilient, and I was able to recover without too many problems. However, I know the strangulation was serious. I still choke easily, especially when I eat something or drink a beverage. It is only by the grace of God I survived.

Beside herself with anger, mom ordered my father out. She managed to cobble together funds for a bus ticket east by collecting the next month's rent in advance from the renters and combining that with some petty cash she kept on hand for emergencies. My father "borrowed" two dollars for lunch meat, cheese, and bread at a nearby store so he could make himself a few sandwiches before going to the bus depot for the long trip to Chicago.

As far as we know, he spent the rest of his life in and out of VA hospitals until he died on April 18, 1961. I hope someone saw him in the VA hospital and helped him turn around his life before it was too late. I have long gotten over the fact that I grew up without my father around for most of my life. Thank goodness for the close friends who helped me through life and gave me the determination to never look back.

Billy and Wade

Pleasant Memories

As I said, a seven-year-old is resilient. So, I also have some pleasant memories of growing up in San Jose. In 1950 the population totaled over 95,000, or less than a tenth of its modern-day size. Kids in the modern, high-tech Silicon Valley environment have no idea what it was like to walk down the street and pick strawberries or pears off nearby trees. Lush prune and apricot fields sat just east of our home.

"Fruit Pickers"

In the 1950s, our San Jose home sat in the middle of an agrarian landscape, referred to by legendary author Jack London as the "Sun-kissed Santa Clara Valley" in his popular adventure story The Call of the Wild. One day, Buzz used our surroundings to hatch a new money-making plan: he and Billy would become fruit pickers. They picked beans and assorted crops until Billy refused to work anymore.

So, Buzz had to develop a new strategy, enticing me to also pick apricots and arouse Billy's curiosity. One morning quite early, a pickup truck stopped by our house. The three of us jumped into the bed as the truck roared

down 4th Street, heading toward an apricot ranch. Too short to maneuver a ladder up the trees, I drew the task of picking cots that had fallen to the ground. It was the lowest of the low.

Meanwhile, Buzz and Billy had fun climbing ladders all day! This routine went on for several days before the rancher either let us go or Buzz moved onto another venture. Either way, Billy was happy. He had quickly tired of the early morning routine and long days of hard work.

—*Brother Wade Howell*

I also have good memories of walking through Saint James Park, whose 6.8 acres sit in the midst of San Jose and date back to its founding in 1777. I think of it as a smaller version of New York's famed Central Park. Mom, my brothers, and I would stroll through Saint James on our way downtown to shop at Hale's Department Store. If we had time, we would also visit the department store where my dad briefly worked. I have memories of having a Coke, lunch, or a milkshake at Woolworths, another legendary name in America's retailing past. It is now a historical memory—except for the Woolworth Building in New York, still one of the nation's fifty tallest.

Billy and I would spend our summer hours at Saint James Park and nearby Ryland Park, where we learned to swim. If we had enough extra change, we would visit one of the two restaurants on 4th Street—a Burger Bar on one corner and a Taco Tico's on the other.

My brother Lynnie (Wade) remembers a funny story from childhood involving the sale of The Mercury News. Selling newspapers was one way my brothers and I made some extra spending money. After school, we would go downtown to sell the afternoon edition, in those days a big deal because it had the latest sports scores. I would make Billy take half of them and walk to the next corner down the street. An extremely good-looking kid, Billy had a complacent attitude about everything and never put forth much effort to sell papers.

"A Ragamuffin Clan"

My mother gave my big brother the absolute worst name in the family: Basil Auvil Howell Jr. She claimed that during World War II, all mothers named their male children after their fathers. According to her, dad was furious when he found out about it. No one ever spoke my brother's middle name out loud, and only mom called him Basil. Everyone else called him Bas, until as a teen-

ager, he decided to change his name to Buzz. Smart move.

As the oldest brother, Buzz was certainly the leader of our little ragamuffin clan, at times dominating my other brother, Billy, and me. We were street urchins roaming around the sleepy town of San Jose. I happily followed Buzz anywhere he allowed me to go.

Buzz decided one day that he would allow me to sell the afternoon newspaper with him and Billy. Distributed every afternoon, the San Jose Mercury News sold for a dime. Naturally, Buzz selected the busiest street corner downtown—First and Santa Clara— as his prime location and placed Billy and me on different corners.

Buzz kept a close eye on the clock so he could march us over to the Food Machinery and Chemical factory at quitting time. We would stand at the gate and wait for workers to exit the building. Then, Buzz would push me out front with a stack of newspapers because I was a little waif of a child.

Once it got too dark to sell newspapers, he would cash us out. We often stopped at Thrifty's Drugstore afterward for a treat: a

marvelous hot fudge sundae with a swirl of whipped cream and bright red cherry.
—*Brother Wade Howell*

After a while, we would all reunite and often put Lynnie out front in a subtle attempt to sell more copies. Just a preschooler, Lynnie was five years younger than me and so cute that people would invariably stop to chat. Not wanting to disappoint the little guy, many would dig into their pockets for spare change. However, when his cuteness didn't seal the deal, I suggested walking over to Julian Street, where a large chemical manufacturing plant was located, to sell our remaining inventory.

By doing this, we sold enough newspapers over one three-month period to rank among the *Mercury News's* top ten sellers. As a reward, our boss took us and other leading sales agents to Alum Rock Park in the back of his truck. No one wore a seatbelt because back then, you could get away with that kind of stuff. We cooked hotdogs over an open fire on sticks and hung out, all the while having too much fun to notice when it got dark. Then our boss took us back home.

Newspapers continued being a part of my life for many years. By the age of eleven, I was getting up at 5:00 a.m. to deliver morning papers, with mom helping me put rubber bands on them so I could toss them into neighbors' yards and still make it to school on time. This early morning routine left me free in the afternoons to be a starting catcher on a baseball team in the Spartan Little League.

On many Saturdays, we three boys headed off at noon for a short stroll through Saint James Park and half a block up 1st Street to the Crest Movie Theater. There we would watch cartoons, movie serials, and a cowboy movie for the princely sum of twenty-five cents. On Sundays, we often went to Saint Patrick's Catholic Church, where all three of us took our first Communion.

Surviving Calamity

As with all kids, childhood included its share of calamities. At the age of nine, I was playing in the front yard with the boy who lived upstairs from us when he threw a rock (or a mud clot; I'm not sure which) that smacked me in the face. I chased him, and he fled upstairs, where he slammed a door that had glass in the top frame. It broke as my right hand hit the wood frame. When my left hand came in contact with the broken glass, the shards sliced my left wrist. The cut began to bleed profusely. To control it, my mother wrapped a towel around the wound and down my left arm. Then she rushed me to the hospital so they could bandage it.

70 YEARS OF GOD'S MIRACLES

The hospital also referred me to a doctor who was one of the few in San Jose who performed skin grafts. I wound up needing a skin graft from my left leg to cover my left wrist. The specialist told me it would be the first one done on a child in San Jose—yet if it wasn't successful, it could leave me with a crippled hand. Since I was so active, the wound broke open a few times, but it finally healed. I thank God the operation was successful, and I didn't lose the use of my left hand. Ironically, because the gash was on the backside of my wrist, I can't see it, but I can see the scar on my left leg.

The same year as my accident, mom (who had divorced my father soon after he attacked me) remarried to a man named Jerry on a quick trip to Reno, Nevada. One of the poker players who lived next door, Jerry, seemed nice enough but was always going out to play cards. His fellow card players nicknamed him "The Deacon" because he would not drink alcohol. We kids even referred to him by his nickname when we answered him.

I remember some trips we made to the boardwalk on Santa Cruz Beach and to the San Francisco Zoo and Playland, a ten-acre seaside amusement park that ultimately closed in 1972. While neither destination was that far away in miles, in pre-interstate days, it could take a long time. The route to San Francisco was the historic El Camino Real, Spanish for "The Royal Road."

It was built centuries ago to connect twenty-one Catholic missions and other facilities along a seven-hundred-mile path. Clogged with traffic and stoplights, it could take two hours or more to travel the fifty-five-mile distance.

While those were good times, I honestly don't have that many memories of Jerry. Since he was always out gambling, we rarely saw him. After less than four years of an absentee husband, mom had had enough too. Before his departure, though, my youngest brother, Jerre, was born, completing our family of four boys. Our mom used to comment she never wanted girls because they would be too much trouble.

Jerre was a happy baby and always had a smile, but he was still a toddler when I entered my teen years, an occasion for dread. As one of the shortest guys in my class who often got picked on, I feared what bullying I might face at a larger school. Now, I didn't know it at the time, but the rock-n-roll era and my fascination with bowling would pull me out of the doldrums.

CHAPTER 3

The Music of Our Lives

"Rejoice in the LORD, O you righteous, for praise is fitting for the upright."

Psalm 33:1 (MEV)

Every generation has its music. Frankly, I can't tell you much about what singers or groups are popular today as we progress through the twenty-first century. Ironically, I feel the same way today that my mother did in the 1950s: I'm not able to understand young people's music, nor why they like it. But just like me as a teen, one reason they like it is that their parents (and grandparents) don't. Some things never change.

Born in 1942, I became a teen just as rock-n-roll was heating up, thanks to the emergence of heartthrob Elvis Presley. Signed in 1954 by Sun Records in Memphis, Tennessee, at the tender age of nineteen, a year later, RCA Victor bought his recording contract. By 1956, Elvis had become an international sensation. He still is several decades after his death in 1977.

Of course, Elvis didn't create this genre all by himself. There were such popular artists as Fats Domino, who in 1955 had a hit with "Ain't That a Shame," also recorded that year by clean-cut crooner Pat Boone. Fats, a bluesy pianist, would strike it rich again in '56 with "Blueberry Hill," originally released during the 1940s. The year before I became a teenager (on August 11, 1955), there were hits like "Pledging My Love" by Johnny Ace; the Penguins' "Earth Angel"; LeVern Baker's "Tweedle Dee"; "I Got a Woman" by the legendary Ray Charles; and "Sincerely" by the Moonglows.

More hits followed in 1955, like "Maybellene" by Chuck Berry; "Blue Suede Shoes" by Carl Perkins; and Johnny Cash's original rendition of "Folsom Prison Blues," which enjoyed a second wave of popularity in 1968, thanks to his live recording at Folsom Prison. The year of '55 also saw "I Hear You Knocking" by Smiley Lewis; future pop star Little Richard's "Tutti Fruitti"; the Platters' "Only You"; "Roll with Me, Henry" by Etta James; and "Bo Diddly," the hit that took its name from the singer who recorded it.

The flood continued in 1956 when Elvis released a 45 RPM recording that contained number one hits on both sides. While RCA billed "Don't Be Cruel" as the A-side, the B track, "Hound Dog," proved equally popular. They alternately held the top slot on the Billboard charts for eleven weeks. Elvis followed up in 1957 with "All Shook Up," which topped Billboard's "Hot 100" for eight weeks, starting in mid-April. If that weren't enough, in '57, the singer would star in two movies—*Loving You* and *Jailhouse Rock*.

That year would see the release of what many consider the most popular classic car, the 1957 Chevy, and another string of musical hits. Among them were "Wake Up Little Susie" by the Everly Brothers; "Dianna," by Paul Anka; "Party Doll" by Buddy Knox; "That'll Be the Day" by Buddy Holly and the Crickets; "Little Darling" by the Diamonds; "Peggy Sue" by Buddy Holly; and "School Day" by Chuck Berry.

Excitement in the Air

I'm not naming all these artists just to take a stroll down Memory Lane, but to emphasize the considerable influence this era had on rescuing my self-image. The hits of my early teens not only touched off the rock-n-roll era, but they also gave me an identity and helped me overcome the low self-esteem that had been a constant companion throughout my youth. As I mentioned in the last chapter, from fourth grade on I was one of the shortest—and skinniest—guys in my class. That's a bit ironic, considering how a pronounced growth spurt in my early twenties finally helped me shoot up to six feet, four inches in height. At one class reunion, women who had once scorned me showed interest, but by then, it was too late. I had my beautiful wife with me.

"The Terrible Trio"

We lived near the local college and often walked to San Jose State for basketball games. One evening, we must have stayed out a little too late; a police car pulled over to the curb as we were walking home. The policeman talked to Buzz for quite a while. The next thing I knew, we were being herded into the backseat of his car—something about a curfew.

I was more bewildered than scared. After all, my big brother was sitting next to me. The policeman drove us home and marched us up the stairs of our shabby, neglected Victorian home. Oddly enough, our mother didn't reprimand us. Thankfully, this was our only brush with the law.

Most days were calmer and more fun. Summers in San Jose could get blistering hot, reaching into the 100s. On those days, the three of us ambled over to the public swimming pool in Ryland Park, clutching our swim trunks inside of a towel. Our path led us across a set of railroad tracks. If we were lucky, there might be a couple of boxcars loaded down with celery stalks. Buzz had no fear. He would climb up the ladder, scramble to the top, reach inside, and grab a stalk. Then he climbed back down, and we continued our walk while he ripped off a rib at a time to share with Billy and me.

At the swimming pool, we would splash around in the water until we were tired out. Then we jumped out of the pool and strategically placed our towels on the hot concrete walkway, careful not to singe our skin too badly. Then we would lay our wet bodies down on the towel to air dry in the sun and proceed to get a vicious sunburn on our collective backs.

—*Brother Wade Howell*

Propelled by a wave of postwar prosperity, the day's popular music created an aura of excitement amongst most of my classmates. What a start to a classic era! You could feel the electricity in the air, with every new artist whose record hit the charts becoming an instant celebrity. They were the talk of Peter Burnett Junior High School, which was named for California's first governor in 1850-1851 when San Jose was the state capital. It was a fantastic time to be a teen. Like so many others, almost every week I was at a nearby record store, buying 45 RPMs (and it is worth noting that in recent years vinyl records have made a huge comeback) and taking them to spin on our record player.

One of our favorite shows aired at 3:00 p.m. daily: *American Bandstand*. It started in 1952 as just *Bandstand*, but in 1957 they hired Dick Clark as the DJ; he would later move the show from Philadelphia to Los Angeles and stay with it until 1989. That show was where I learned to dance. All the new dance styles originated on the program, and recording artists appeared on it to sing their hit songs. By my senior year in high school, it had twenty million viewers. Though broadcast in black and white in those days, watching a show directed at teens added to the thrills of our music scene.

When my brothers and I weren't watching *American Bandstand*, we were wearing out many of the 45s in my sizable collection. I was able to afford these records because of my paper route and a weekend job selling peanuts at San Jose Municipal Stadium, today known as Excite Ballpark. I would ride my bike to the stadium, which since the 1940s has been home to a succession of minor league baseball teams with various major league affiliations. The gentleman who ran the concession must have liked the way I yelled out, "get your red hots here!" or "anyone need some peanuts?" At least, I assumed he did since he would sometimes take me and a couple of other concessionaires to Saturday night hot rod races.

I reveled in the feelings of popularity that I sensed with customers in the stands yelling their appreciation or laughing together with my fellow sales vendors at the races. On campus, I was a short shrimp and far from popular. One time in seventh grade, as I walked from gym class back to the main building with a group of students, a guy in another group walking our way cold-cocked me on the chin. I went down and came back up with a sore jaw.

That humiliation summarizes my early teenage status. Since I never dated or went to school dances, I found escape in rock-n-roll records and the other activity whose popularity would soar during the 1950s and '60s: bowling.

Competing for Cash

As a late bloomer, much of my social life in those days consisted of visiting 4th Street Bowl, located just a quick bike ride up the street from our house. I joined the junior bowling league with my brother Billy. We bowled as much as we could, including almost every day in the summer. By the age of seventeen, I was good enough to bowl in an adult league, with my averages hovering in the 190 to 200 range. My skills grew to the point I bowled against others for money and became a formidable opponent. Thanks to the tables at the alley, I learned to shoot pool too, and would play games of nine-ball or straight pool for cash.

One time while bowling for money, I rolled a 300. By then, a senior in high school, I worked on the San Jose High School newspaper, *The Bulldog News*. When I told the editor about my perfect game, he put a story in the next issue, and my achievement was announced in all of the classrooms the next morning. Thanks to this notoriety, a flock of my classmates soon started showing up at the 4th Street Bowl, making it *the* place to hang out.

Four guys from those days became lifelong friends of Billy and me: Nick and Marshall Mendez, Larry Newman, and Hector Rodriguez. Larry ended up being better at playing pool than me, but I still came out ahead. The rule was that if one of us played an opponent and won our match, that guy had to pay for his friends' meals. So, Larry bought us lots of food.

The 4th Street pool room became a major place for excellent pool players, like Dick McMoran and others who hailed from all over California. Known around the area as "San Jose Dick" because of his skills, Dick worked in San Jose and would come in occasionally on weekends to play pool. If some hotshot came in looking to play against him, I would do a little screening, asking what game he wanted to play and for how much money. Then I'd tell the guy I would call Dick to see if he was available.

As the pool room grew in popularity, increasing numbers of people came to play or just hang out. The games were usually for big money in those days; you could pick up anywhere from fifty to two hundred bucks in total winnings for the night. When a pool shark from Los Angeles named Richie Allen showed up to play, and word got out, the crowds mushroomed to the point that no one could play at the other five tables. One time when Allen showed up, I got a hold of Dick McMoran, and he rushed down to play. Dick was one of three or four hustlers who could play for high stakes; sometimes the money was his, but often people would offer him up to a thousand dollars to play with in return for a cut of the winnings. These kinds of matches went on until the wee hours of the morning, with most of the action at night and on weekends. We would play or watch until the next morning.

Cast of Characters

In addition to "San Jose Dick," Billy gave other pool sharks and bowling alley rats colorful nicknames that added to the festive atmosphere. There was "Firecracker Frank," "Rat Hole Pete," "Santa Clara John," "Parking Lot Benny," and "Zombie."

Firecracker Frank was from Miami, Florida. He got his nickname from his habit of running through the bowling alley and tossing small firecrackers at people's feet before dashing out the other side of the alley. If it had happened only once, it wouldn't have been such a big deal, but Frank continued pulling this prank for several months. Whenever we heard crackling noises erupting, we shrugged and said: "It's just Firecracker Frank."

Rathole Pete was from Oakland. He often played at another pool hall he colorfully dubbed "The Rat Hole." As you can surmise from his name, San Jose Dick lived in San Jose and was the best pool player in the city. Likewise, Santa Clara John was from just down the road in Santa Clara. He too was a great pool player. Parking Lot Benny derived his nickname from his hot temper. If things didn't go his way, he would often call people out to the parking lot to fight it out. You can probably guess the origin of Zombie. The guy would take so many pills that he acted and talked like one. However, when sober, Zombie was a pretty intelligent guy.

A character known as "San Francisco Junior Bateman" liked to give people hotfoots. The front door of 4th Street Bowl was next to the pool room, with a shoeshine stand about ten feet from the door. Late at night, someone would often try to catch a catnap on one of the shoeshine stand chairs. Every so often, San Francisco Junior would pour lighter fluid on their shoes and light them with a match before running away. The victim usually woke up and quickly stamped out the flames, but one night the guy didn't wake up soon enough to put out the fire and wound up in the hospital. San Francisco Junior never got arrested, though. No one would rat him out.

While most of the billiard's action took place at 4th Street Bowl, after I was old enough to drive, some friends and I would set out on Saturday for neighboring cities. We played at different pool halls or searched for a bowling alley where we could challenge other bowlers for money. One time I drove up to San Francisco with Dick McMoran to watch him play some high-stakes games at Cochran's Billiards. The legendary pool hall was about three miles south of Fisherman's Wharf. Cochran's had a colorful history with nicknames for the sharpshooters who frequented the place, like "One-Eyed Hank," "Mexican Phil," "Okie Sam," and "Sleepy Bob."

The players also knew about San Jose Dick, who liked the action so much he sometimes rented two tables next to each other so he could play two opponents simultaneously. At one time, Dick had the reputation as one of the best One Pocket players around. In that game, whoever breaks the rack shoots to put as many as possible in the left corner while the other guy takes the right side corner. Given Dick's skill and reputation, I figured I could profit handsomely by giving him some cash as part of his stake that night. Although he started out winning, during his streak, he started drinking and lost his edge. Consequently, Dick wound up losing all the money I had given him to wager. Naturally, I have some bad memories of Cochran's.

Colorful Escapades

Billy and I had our share of other escapades. Along with a friend named Marshall, we liked to tie a fake hundred-dollar bill to a long string and put it by the door. Then we would hide behind some vending machines about thirty to forty feet away. When someone would come through the door, see the bill, and bend over in an effort to pick up the bill, we would yank on the string. People would often keep stretching further, sometimes cussing when they were unable to pick up the C note. Meanwhile, we kept our mouths covered with a hand, trying to muffle our laughter.

One of Billy's favorite stories concerned Junior Bateman, who used to live in Sacramento. He and some friends liked to visit that city's J Street, in those days known as "Restaurant Row." Junior and his buddies would order expensive steak dinners and then slip out the door without paying. Invariably, as they were leaving, someone would scream, "They're leaving without paying the bill!" That sent Junior and his pals in a mad dash down J Street.

Billy decided to bring the phrase and the practice of ordering meals without paying for them to our area. Although they succeeded in getting free meals several times, that came to an end after a trip to neighboring Sunnyvale. When they "J Streeted" an establishment, the owner and two men ran after them, pursuing them all the way into a fruit orchard. One of Billy's friends lost his footing, fell, and got apprehended. Taking him back to the restaurant by the scruff of his neck, the trio ordered him to either pay the bill in full or they would call the police.

Given their laid-back demeanor and affection for shooting the breeze, Billy, Nick, Marshall, and Hector all became barbers while Larry and I went into the car business. These stories and many more continued to make us laugh throughout our lives and created life-long bonds between us.

"A Storybook Life"

Way back in the 1980s, I was watching a TV show with dad when he noticed someone onscreen whom he swore had worked

at his favorite teenage hangout, 4th Street Bowl. He told me the guy had worked at the desk handling customers as a way of earning extra money during his studies at San Jose State College. The desk clerk had told him that after graduation, he was heading for Hollywood. It sounded so other-worldly, like it came out of a storybook, that I wasn't sure I believed it.

Still, I enjoyed the character the former 4th Street Bowl clerk was portraying. He seemed a bit of a scatterbrain as he scrambled through paperwork, scribbling on paper, napkins, and what-not as he tried to get things in order, only to be at it again the next day. Yet, I grew a bit irritated with Dad's interruptions while he was comparing the actor to the character. At one point, my father declared: "He might make it as a writer, but not as an actor."

Dad kept talking until it was almost time for that episode to end. Later, I teased him by imitating the actor's manner of speaking. At the time, I didn't recognize my own passive-aggressive behavior.

What I realize today is that my behavior toward my father was unfair. My dad was

having trouble telling me this actor was in person because of the character he portrayed. I should have given him more slack because I have found myself in the same predicaments. I guess you could say: like father, like son.

—*Son Gavin Howell*

Change of Scenery

After graduating from high school, in 1961 I enrolled in San Jose City College. My mother wanted me to study engineering, thinking it represented a good future. After a tough start, I switched majors to business and found my true calling. My mentor was a professor named Ross Atkinson. In addition to my classes, I joined the debate club and traveled to many other colleges for debate competitions, which our team usually won. To make money for school, I worked part-time at the 4th Street Bowl.

However, I had to leave school at the end of 1963 to fulfill my military obligations. I had enlisted in the California National Guard, and it was time to report to Fort Ord. Located about sixty miles south of San Jose along the coast of Monterey Bay, at the time, it was considered one of the army's most beautiful bases. During my six months of active duty, I gained about thirty pounds and grew about three inches in height.

After six weeks of training, an outbreak of meningitis hit the new barracks up the hill from ours. At the time, the disease was lethal and lingered for two years, with the army later deciding to close that post. Basic training lasted eight weeks and after it ended, we finally got a weekend off. I snagged a ride to San Jose that Friday. The next day my old buddy, Larry Newman, took me to pick up my 1956 Cadillac from my ex-girlfriend's house. She had sent me a "Dear John" letter four weeks earlier.

When I returned to Fort Ord to complete my final four months of Guard duty, I met John Moller while we were both on sick call. John and I became lifelong friends. One of our favorite outings was to a nightclub a few miles away from the base. They sponsored a dance contest every Thursday night. One time I picked up a nice-looking lady and won the $100 contest and a trophy. The judges ended up giving her both prizes, and I never saw her again.

Troubled Time

My time in the Guard ultimately led to a firsthand look at the 1965 Watts Riots, a unique event in American history, with multiple fires set and forty million dollars in property damage resulting from the chaos. Racial tensions erupted after a California Highway Patrol officer pulled over a twenty-one-year-old motorist one Wednesday night at 116th street and Avalon Boulevard for reckless driving. The driver, Marquette Frye, failed the sobriety test, but as it proceeded, a crowd of about fifty people slowly gathered. Tensions rose, and when his mother showed up, she began cursing and shouting they would have to kill him to take him to jail. The CHP officers attempted to handcuff Frye, but he resisted. His mother, Rena, jumped onto an officer's back. According to the state report, an officer swung his baton at Marquette Frye's shoulder but missed and struck him in the head, causing bleeding.

Witnesses told others in the crowd that police had abused Rena Frye, although she later told the *Los Angeles Times* that was not true. Still, the crowd soon swelled to nearly a thousand people as Marquette, stepbrother Ronald, and their mother were all taken away in handcuffs. After the Fryes were detained, police arrested a man and woman in the crowd on allegations they had incited violence. A rumor quickly spread that the woman was pregnant and had been abused by the arresting officers. This claim was untrue, according to the 101-page McCone Commission Report issued months later.

Still, on that hot summer night, the crowd erupted in a fury. People began throwing rocks at police cruisers as the crowd broke off into smaller groups. Caucasian motorists in the area were pulled from their cars and beaten, and store windows were smashed. A second round of riots erupted on the next night as seven thousand people took to the streets and spread chaos in Watts and surrounding South Los Angeles neighborhoods. About seventy-five people were injured, including thirteen police officers. Dozens of buildings along Avalon Boulevard were burned. Reports surfaced that rioters were stealing machetes and rifles from pawnshops. Firefighters attempting to douse blazes throughout the neighborhood had to take cover when people began shooting at them. Ultimately, thirty-four people lost their lives, and one thousand were injured.

California's lieutenant governor called in the National Guard. By Saturday night, a curfew had been set, and nearly fourteen thousand troops were patrolling a forty-six-mile area. What I remember about that time was leaving San Jose's training facility in military trucks in full gear and traveling to Southern California for more than ten hours. We arrived at a grade school and slept on the floor during the daytime. Around 6:00 p.m., we had to get ready with our rifles fully loaded to arrive at Watts by their curfew time.

The police chief instructed us that if we saw anyone out or around the area, we were to shoot to kill. The few days and nights we were deployed, we rode around the streets in military trucks, with all our rifles pointed toward buildings, apartments, homes, and businesses. Thankfully, our unit never needed to fire a shot. A few days later, we traveled back to San Jose, so exhausted we needed a few days' sleep.

The Right to Vote

One of the great rights that many young adults take for granted is the right to vote when they turn eighteen; during the 1960s, the voting age was twenty-one. So, I just missed voting for the youngest, best-looking, and most charismatic man to ever run for president, John F. Kennedy. I remember all the people my age who also couldn't vote for him. We were struck with sorrow over his assassination by Lee Harvey Oswald less than three years into his first term in office. Those were tragic days to live through; I believe nearly everyone, at one time or another, cried their eyes out. Eventually, the tears stop, but the pain lingers. I like to focus on the good times whenever I watch old pictures or video highlights that occasionally appear on a TV program. The press started to call this time the loss of America's innocence. That was true for me.

Kennedy was president from January 20, 1961, until his unfortunate assassination on November 22, 1963. At forty-three, he was the second-youngest president ever elected. The author of the legendary *Profiles in Courage*, Kennedy, was the only president to have won a Pulitzer Prize, as well as the first Catholic to hold the office. His short-lived presidency saw numerous landmark events:

the building of the Berlin Wall, the Cuba missile crisis, the ill-fated Bay of Pigs invasion, increased involvement in the Vietnam War, the onset of the space race, and the early days of the equal rights movement.

Vice President Lyndon B. Johnson ascended to the presidency after Kennedy's death and remained there until January 20, 1969. Johnson was one of four presidents to have served in all major federal elected offices of the US government. He was president, vice president, a congressional representative, and a senator during his career. LBJ was well known for his policies, including supporting the civil rights movement, formation of Medicare and Medicaid, and the Public Broadcasting System; launching the War on Poverty; aid to education; and advancing environmental protections. However, his foreign strategy with the Vietnam War dragged down his popularity and ultimately forced Johnson from office.

Roller Coaster of Sales

After my six months in the National Guard, I decided to go to work, joining the sales force at San Jose Ford on Market Street. The dealership trained me to know all about Ford products, including how to sell vehicles by starting at the front and circling around the car. I also learned how to do demonstration drives and make friends with customers. As a brand-new salesman, the dealership put me on a team with a person who helped us close deals. Once the customer selected a car, I went to the desk with the written offer and introduced the customer to the sales manager.

"A Blessed Life"

As a teen, Buzz earned enough money (collectively!) to buy a new portable record player, something that proved to be a life-changing event. Soon 1950s rock-and-roll music screamed into our living room: Little Richard's "Good Golly Miss Molly"; Elvis Presley's double-sided hits "Hound Dog" and Don't Be Cruel"; Jerry Lee Lewis' "Whole Lot of Shaking Going On"; Fats Domino's "Blueberry Hill"; and Buddy Holly's "That'll Be the Day." Every day Buzz brought home a new forty-five record; it filled the house with excitement. Even at an early age, he had the ability to make life better for all of us.

My oldest brother went on to other equally successful endeavors. After embarrassingly failing his senior year, he went back for an extra year of high school to graduate. Buzz then enrolled in San Jose City College and majored in business, working every summer in a cannery to support himself. He finally entered the car business as a novice car salesman after selling knives door-to-door. The car business resonated with Buzz. He worked his way through all the various managerial positions and ended his career as general manager and part-owner of a dealership.

Although successful in his chosen career, his real success was in maintaining childhood friendships, creating new and lifelong friendships, and centering his attentions on a loving family. Buzz had gumption, grit, dogged determination, tenacity, spunk, and ambition—all old-fashioned terms that still resonate. He not only changed his name; he changed the direction of his life. He was going to do better than the cards dealt to him as a youngster.

Buzz imbued a real sense of charisma. I would witness men talking to my brother, getting physically close enough and then touching his shirt sleeve as if they could capture some magical fairy dust from him. Without a doubt, my brother faced some crushing financial losses and deeply personal heartaches, but always, Buzz would say his

life was blessed. I still believe him when he says it now.

—Brother Wade Howell

Even though I was a beginner, all of my college sales training kicked in. I quickly became one of the top three in monthly sales. Six months later, I moved to Bob Sykes Dodge on Stevens Creek in Santa Clara, using all my sales skills to move plenty of new and used vehicles.

By early summer of 1965, our National Guard unit went to A-1 status, which meant instead of one weekend of training a month, we had to go twice. Our weekend training would start at 6:00 p.m. on Friday night, traveling from San Jose to Fort Ord in military trucks. Proceeding at slow speeds and taking fifteen- to twenty-minute breaks along the way, we usually arrived around midnight. On Saturdays, we trained for combat for ten to twelve hours. On Sunday, we trained from 8:00 a.m. to 6:00 p.m. before taking the military truck back to San Jose and arriving around midnight.

While I started out with a great track record at Sykes Dodge, things slowly started to sink. After three months of my sales decreasing by 50 percent and management ready to let me go, I called John Moller, my sick call buddy from Fort Ord. John lived in Azusa, not far from Los Angeles. Along with his father and two brothers, John owned two USA Gas stations and a three-bedroom home. He immediately invited me to share the space. I lived in one of the bedrooms, while John and his brother, Finn, occupied the other two. I moved into their home in January of 1966. John also worked out a transfer for me to a National Guard tank unit in Pasadena. After I left San Jose, the National Guard froze transfers so no one else could leave. The San Jose soldiers trained two weekends a month for another two years but were never sent to Vietnam.

CHAPTER 4

The Love of My Life

"He who finds a wife finds a good thing, and obtains favor from the LORD."

Proverbs 18:22

My first job in Southern California was with T. Lyell Puckett Ford in Alhambra, a truly old-style car dealership. Because it was six miles from famed Santa Anita Park, on race day, almost all the salesmen and managers went to watch the horses. As he headed out the door, the sales manager would toss me the keys and call: "You're in charge, kid." I only lasted a few months there because the dealership hardly advertised, which meant not many new customers came through the doors.

If someone showed up, they usually asked for a salesperson they had worked with on a previous purchase. The only way I ever managed to sell a car is if someone called the number I had on flyers, which I placed on the windshields of cars in the area. Or, I might luck out on one of the telephone cold calls I made nearly every day. So, I quit and took a job at Downey Ford, about twenty miles from Azusa.

While that first job didn't work out, as far as my personal life, the move to Azusa was the best I ever made. I loved Mexican food; John told me the best Mexican restaurant around was La Tolteca on Azusa Avenue, not far from his home. One Sunday afternoon, when I went to the counter for the first time, the most beautiful Mexican girl I had ever seen took my order. After asking for my favorite dish, chile verde, I asked the clerk—named Esperanza—and her friend, Yolanda, what they did for fun and excitement. They told me there were plenty of places to go dancing and exciting parties, as well as a bowling alley.

Fascinated by her appearance and manner, I asked Esperanza for a date the next day. Her immediate response: "I don't date 'gringos,'" Hispanic slang for white guys. I quickly responded, "Well, I'm half-Mexican." When I said that, she agreed to a date. Since she worked Mondays, she said Tuesday would be better because that was her day off. I immediately took out the small address book I carried and jotted down her address. She told me to pick her up at 4:00 p.m.

Tuesday couldn't come soon enough. I drove to her home and honked the horn. Soon the front door opened, with Espe stepping out and waving me inside her parents' house. At that time, I didn't know that Espe had told her parents I was half-Mexican and half white, as I had told her at La Tolteca. I lied because I already knew that most Mexican women wouldn't date gringos.

Ethnic Clash

I had firsthand experience with the clash between gringos and Mexicans through my old pool hall buddies, Larry Newman (also white) and Mexicans Nick and Marshall Mendez. As teens, Larry and I often went to the Mendez house for gatherings and meals. That is until Marshall went into the army. One day we stopped by at lunchtime for some of Kay's fantastic Mexican food. She refused, saying, "I'm not going to feed you while my son is away."

Hurt, Larry, and I decided to picket her house. We left and made up signs that read, "Unfair to Gringos!" When we returned later, we paraded back and forth outside, holding our signs high. A neighbor across the street called and told her what was happening in front of her house. Soon, she burst through the door and yelled at us.

"We're staying until you feed us," we replied.

Shaking her head, she yelled, "get in here, gringos!"

Every time we met at a social gathering after that, she always shared that story.

Through a series of friendships growing up, I had learned a lot about Mexican culture and felt completely at home with them. I especially loved the food and backyard parties at the Mendez family's home. I also liked the feelings of acceptance and love I felt there, which compensated for the lack of affection I sensed at my own house. I've always felt more comfortable with Mexican women. Since I had told a few Mexican girls I dated that I was half-Mexican, I didn't feel I was stretching the truth too far with Espe.

Though she didn't learn about my deceit for a long time, Espe had a surprise waiting for me. Right after I sat down on their couch, she said, "I have a confession to make. I'm not a party girl and need to be chaperoned on dates."

I sat there for about ten minutes as Espe ticked off all the rules she had to follow. Then she stood up and walked toward the front door, which I took as my signal to leave. Still sitting, mired in thought with my hands holding up my chin, I finally arose and said, "I will try it." She called to her siblings to go for a ride with us. We went to a miniature golf course that day, and everyone had a great time.

Storybook Romance

Our second date was a bit inspired. The Sound of Music had premiered in April of 1965 but was just making a major splash in the Hollywood area. That included a showing at the notable (though now closed) Fox Wilshire Theater in Beverly Hills, less than five miles from Hollywood. I invited Espe to go on her next day off, the ninth of February. She asked her parents, and they finally agreed she could go if she were home by eleven o'clock. No chaperones needed. We thoroughly enjoyed the movie, and I bought Espe a souvenir book that she still treasures. On the way home, the radio played "Strangers in the Night" by Frank Sinatra; the song meant a lot to Espe because she related the lyrics to us.

After our date at *The Sound of Music*, I would often stop by Espe's after work. I enjoyed spending time with her while we played with her little sister and her brother. Espe would also interpret for me in conversations with her parents, who only spoke Spanish. We got along very well. By this time, Espe had befriended or dated several dozen guys, with four of them offering her an engagement ring. Her aunt used to say, "Changes boyfriends like we change shoes."

Espe and I had many dates with her little sister and brother along, at drive-in movies, Coffee Dan's, or swimming at John Moller's home, where I taught them how to swim. Espe and I were engaged on April Fool's Day of 1966. However, on July 22, Espe angrily threw her engagement ring on the front lawn at John's home. She had just gotten off the phone with a friend of mine, who had boldly tried to make a move on her. Apologizing, I begged for her forgiveness. I was in love and impulsively brought up the idea of driving to Las Vegas right then to get married. Although she agreed, it took her several minutes to find the ring on John's lawn.

After I had packed my clothes, we drove to Espe's home. When we told her parents, they gave us their approval. We then went to John's father's home to borrow one of his cars; the new Ford I was driving was owned by Downey Ford, and I couldn't drive it out of the area. John's father offered to drive us, but his wife talked him out of it, persuading him that we wanted to get married by ourselves. After he graciously lent me his car, we left for Las Vegas at 8:00 p.m. Three flat tires later, we pulled into Las Vegas at 4:00 a.m.

We checked into a downtown motel on July 23, 1966. After obtaining our license at the courthouse, we got married at Cupid's Chapel. Looking back, it all sounds so crazy and foolhardy, a romantic lark ultimately destined for failure. But fifty years later, with a flock of family and relatives looking on, we renewed our vows in that same chapel.

Rude Awakening

Once Espe and I were married, I called my mother while we were still in Las Vegas, telling her I had fallen in love with a beautiful Mexican girl named Espe and we had just gotten married.

"Get an annulment," she replied. That felt like getting cold water thrown in my face. Mom added a few choice words about my decision to cross ethnic boundaries.

Who is she to offer me advice about a mate, considered her two failed marriages? I thought when I finally hung up, sadness written all over my face. When I told Espe about my mother's remarks, she said, "What is your mother talking about? Isn't she a Mexican?"

Oops. Lies always have a way of rearing up to bite you where it hurts. I had to confess that I had lied when we first met. Shocked to learn the truth, she expressed aloud her thoughts about what she should—or could—do. Eventually, I said that I was truly sorry for lying to her when we met. But, I told her, I knew if I had told her the truth, my chances of getting a date with her were zero.

"Well, it's too late now," she finally said. "We have to make it work."

The drive back to Azusa was pretty quiet, with the stillness punctuated by me begging for forgiveness. "I'm so sorry, but I always wanted to marry a beautiful Mexican girl," I said, hoping my explanation would break down the barriers my deceit and my mother's harsh words had erected. "I always had Mexican friends, and their family structure was so beautiful. The families I knew showed me a lot of love, the kind I didn't have at home."

Espe finally calmed down. Then she told me how hurt she felt because I had fit in so well at backyard parties with her parents, extended family, and friends. How I treated Espe's little sister and brother was so special. That even her grandparents on her mother's side (the toughest customers of all) had liked me.

Espe's grandparents: Enrique and Petra Troncoso

She said her dad used to tell her, "The right man to marry will be accepted by the children," and indeed, her little sister and brother loved being around me.

They knew I cared for them because I used to make them laugh, often by poking fun at myself. I had lost my front teeth at the age of eleven when a friend ran into my bike, and his head hit my mouth. So, when we went to Coffee Dan's, I would pull out my front teeth dentures and plop them into Espe's coffee, which provoked considerable laughter. I also took them along to shopping centers, car rides to the mountains, to county fairs, and miniature golf. As we talked things out returning to Azusa, I reminded Espe of these outings, which helped soothe her feelings.

Wedding Day

One of the promises I made to Espe's parents was that we would get married in the Catholic church. Having gone to services at St. Patrick's as a kid, that was fine with me. So, about two months after our Las Vegas nuptials, we were married in a formal ceremony at San Gabriel Mission near Los Angeles. It dated back to 1771. Though a bit small, its tasteful furnishings, narrow windows along a prominent side wall, and six bells cast in Mexico City gave it a historic appearance that added to the special nature of our wedding day.

Espe's cousin, Albert, picked me up at the apartment where we lived in Azusa while Espe was at her parents' home, getting ready. My brother Billy came in from San Jose to be at our wedding, with John Moller serving as my best man. Espe's maid of honor was Cousin Albert's wife, Yvonne. It was a beautiful, sun-drenched afternoon, the kind that everyone wants for their wedding.

Espe looked fantastic in her white gown. Beside her, as bridesmaids were her best friend Yvonne, her aunt Gina, her cousins Florence and Yolanda, and a friend that lived next door. As we watched them all walk down the aisle, I commented to John: "She looks beautiful in her white gown." Once the priest said, "you are now man and wife," her parents felt relieved and were happy we did it "the right way." The flock of family members and friends who attended were happy for us and wished us a long life together. Sadly, my mother wasn't among them, although when she later met Espe, she agreed Espe was lovely and different. And since we're heading toward fifty-five years together, I think our marriage is going to last.

For our reception, we rented a reception hall in Azusa. We had a great time, with everyone having a ball dancing, chatting, and making new friends—like

Espe's sister Emma and my brother Billy. The band played songs from the 1950s and early '60s, which even then we called the "oldies." They also played some current hits too, such as "When a Man Loves a Woman" by Percy Sledge, which was released a few months before our wedding and went straight to number one. It was our song; we requested it three times. For us, it will always be a day to remember.

Back to San Jose

Esperanza continued working at La Tolteca while I stayed on at Downey Ford. However, the next few months were a struggle financially. December brought the last straw; my paycheck for the first two weeks was less than two hundred dollars. When I got home that night, I told Espe, "pack up because we're going to have to move to San Jose." We arrived late that night and checked into a motel. The next day I secured a job at Bob Sykes Dodge, where I had worked before heading to Azusa. The day after that, I rented an apartment on Julian Street, close to San Jose High School.

I had worked previously at Sykes' used car lot down the street. This time I went to the main location with major footage on Stevens Creek Boulevard, a few blocks down from Valley Fair Mall. Despite the retail apocalypse that has claimed numerous victims lately, Valley Fair is still humming along, although now named

Westfield Valley Fair. Stevens Creek had a reputation as "auto row." All the car dealers were there in the area, including Chevrolet, Volkswagen, Dodge, Pontiac, Buick, Mercedes, Volvo, Lincoln-Mercury, Ford, and Chrysler-Plymouth. Most were number one in new car sales in Northern California.

While the owner at Sykes Dodge took a liking to me, the general manager always wanted to challenge me. Chuck dressed like a men's high-fashion model, with a flamboyant style and attitude to match. Since I had a couple of years of automotive experience, they made me a team leader (known as a "closer"), with a team of five young or new salesmen. I spent many hours training my crew on how to sell cars—the first point: make a friend.

Despite my position as a team leader, Chuck usually gave me a bad time about small stuff. He had a good friend on another team and would always favor them. One weekend, Chuck organized the biggest sales contest I ever heard of: $1,000, starting Friday and ending Monday. The top team won it all. Going into the last day, our team was ahead by twelve sales. But when our shift started at 3:00 p.m., we discovered Chuck had credited the other team with fifteen cars. Since they had been sold to a used car dealer at wholesale prices, I felt that violated the rules. When I protested, Chuck replied, "Tough luck! Go to work and sell cars."

Winning the Contest

I gathered my crew together and told them we needed to sell at least three cars to tie the other team. As the clock neared midnight, most of the staff and sales managers waited around to see the final results: we had sold three cars each, A TIE! Chuck said to split the money, but I replied, "I'm going to walk the lot one more time and see if a customer wandered onto the lot." When I reached the wholesale lot, I found a man stealing parts off a vehicle. I told him I was making a citizen's arrest; he asked what he could do to change my mind, and I replied: "Buy a car."

We walked around the lot and found the lowest-priced vehicle. After going for a test drive, we came back and wrote up the deal. I filled out his credit information and brought everything to the sales desk. Guess what? Perfect credit. We won by one sale.

Chuck had a giant plastic bag hanging from the ceiling with 1,000 one-dollar bills. Everyone cheered as we split up the money. I came back to our apartment, threw my share on the bed, and celebrated with Espe. We needed that cash! The next day Chuck said he respected me. From that point on, he was always honest and fair with me until I left Sykes Dodge in 1968. He left soon after and established a successful wholesale business by selling cars bought at wholesale from auctions and through dealerships.

Chuck and I remained friends after going our separate ways. Later, when I worked for Autocar Europe Volvo, I bought some vehicles from him and sold some to him as well. When I took a job in San Francisco, we used to enjoy going to Warrior basketball games together, especially in 1975 when they won the championship.

However, before leaving Sykes, a bigger change affected our lives. After our church wedding at San Gabriel Mission, we learned Espe was a few months pregnant. While everything went smoothly on all of her visits to Doctor Scott, that wasn't the story after we arrived at San Jose Hospital on March 20, 1967. Espe went into labor for twenty hours and was in so much pain she finally tried to get out of bed. The nurse reacted by slapping her, which brought Espe back to reality.

Soon after, Charlene Jean Howell came into the world. After nurses had cleaned her up, the most beautiful baby girl I had ever seen arrived in Espe's room. We were all so happy and excited. Over the next few days, I would stop by after work to see Espe and our beautiful daughter.

We were still living at the apartment on Julian Street. When Espe and Charlene came home, thrills ran through me. I felt so in love! I would carry our little daughter all over the place as I enjoyed her smiling and giggling. Whenever we were having lunch or dinner, I would roll her bassinet over close to me, just to watch her and tickle her chin. Charlene became the second great love of my life.

Welcoming a Newcomer

About sixty days after Charlene's birth, Espe's sister Emma came to stay with us and search for a job. Soon after, she started dating my brother Billy, whom she met at our wedding. Billy picked up Emma at the airport when she flew into San Jose. While Espe was used to the sounds of a newborn, the people who lived under us kept complaining to the manager about our baby's crying, and Espe walking around all the time as she tried to comfort Charlene.

Ironically, Charlene would prove to be a fantastic baby. She constantly smiled, a reflection of her happy character. Whenever we went out, she would giggle and smile. Whenever Espe took her to the supermarket, others would comment how well-behaved and pretty Charlene was for her age. When we went to parks or friends' homes, Charlene was always well-behaved. She loved being outdoors so she could enjoy the sunshine and being around other babies.

However, the complaints from our downstairs neighbors soon after Charlene's birth painted a much different picture. They upset Espe so badly that we finally decided to buy a house so we wouldn't have to worry about such irritations. I called a Realtor I knew, an older gentleman who had just purchased a car from me and had an office six blocks from the dealership. On my next day off, Espe, baby Charlene, and I spent the whole day looking for a house. Finally, we found a nice three-bedroom home.

When the Realtor went to write up the offer at 8:00 p.m., he said, "how much can you put down with the offer?" We looked at each other and said: "Zero." Laughing, he said, "I'll put down a thousand dollars for an offer, and you can cover the down payment at the close of escrow." I turned into a workaholic for the next thirty days, but I sold enough cars to raise the extra thousand dollars we needed by closing. We moved into our new home a week later, with a limited inventory of furniture and belongings. But furnishings didn't matter. We were joyful over the happy realization that we were homeowners, free from the drawbacks of renting.

Just three months later, Espe's mother called, saying she missed her daughters so much. In addition, she and Espe's father (Alberto) were being harassed by their daughter's ex-husband. They soon sold their home in Azusa, and we drove down to rent a moving truck. After loading their furniture, clothing, and other belongings, I drove the rental truck to San Jose. Espe and her sister drove our car, and Alberto, his wife, and their son Eddie followed in their car.

After a few months of living in tight spaces, Espe's mom said she wanted to use the money they had received from the sale of their home in Azusa to buy another home in San Jose where we could all live. I told her my day off was the next day and offered to help look for a bigger house. We ended up at some new homes in the Vista Park area, where we found a two-story house with five bedrooms that was nearly completed. We put our home up for sale and sold it about the same time the new house was ready.

Changing Dealerships

My sales career paralleled our personal lives. Six months after Charlene's birth, I changed dealerships again, joining the sales staff at All-American Pontiac/GMC on North First Street, a block from the 101 freeway. While not as many dealerships as on Stevens Creek, there were several car dealers nearby. Next to All-American were Chrysler/Plymouth and Ford dealerships, while a Chevrolet dealer was four blocks south.

Two blocks to the east of the Chevrolet store was 4th Street Bowl, making me feel like I had come full circle in life. Despite all the great memories, there was no time or money for bowling or games of pool. Still, it was a great move because I reconnected with my old pal Larry Newman, who was selling office furniture and later joined me at another car dealership. At All-American

Pontiac, I made a new friend John Vandenberg, who, with his wife, Nelleke, became lifelong friends. John later worked for me when I became general manager at Don Lucas Cadillac in San Francisco.

Another friend from those days was Bob Rausch, All-American's used car manager. Because of Bob's mentoring, I took a liking to used cars during my time there. He gave me excellent advice on how to buy and merchandise vehicles on the used car lot.

After Bob left, I became the used car manager at All-American and kept up the same sales pace. One great way Bob helped me before leaving was by introducing me to all the new car dealers from the region who sold him their trade-in vehicles. Everything was going well until the General Motors (GM) strike started on September 24, 1969, and lasted for more than four months.

Prior to the strike, I had met with John Chaffetz, the owner of All-American, to go over what would happen if the GM strike did come to pass. With a modest monthly salary of a thousand dollars, most of my pay originated with sales bonuses. When I asked for a guarantee of fifteen hundred a month, and he replied coldly: "If I lose money, you lose money."

Two days later, Bob Rausch called and offered me a sales manager's job at Autocar Europe Volvo, where he had become general manager-used car manager. His boss was Don Lucas, who had been Chaffetz's partner;

Don sold back his stock in All-American to buy the Volvo dealership. I accepted Bob's offer and left after giving All-American one week's notice.

Moving Up

So, in no time at all, I was working at Autocar Europe Volvo. Fortunately, my new boss was someone I really admired and respected as a great person and excellent sales manager and trainer. With me on board, Bob Rausch could take time to visit new car dealers around the peninsula to purchase used import vehicles. In those days, American car dealerships didn't want "foreign" vehicles on their lots. We placed them on our used car lot, where they sold like hotcakes.

This move showed the kind of genius Bob possessed. I absorbed everything he had to say about how to work car sales on the desk and how to motivate and train sales staff. The tip that would last a lifetime: how to value a used vehicle, look over the car for any prior damage, and whether everything fits properly. The inside of the vehicle was also important. Bob also taught me to make sure the interior didn't show any tears or signs of wear and to check to see if the engine ran properly. Did the trunk have any damage or lack a spare tire? Did the tires show much wear? In other words, do a complete check with no shortcuts.

Thanks to such attention to detail and a reputation for honesty and fairness, we enjoyed great success. Bob took the dealership to number one in sales for that Volvo zone, as well as selling two to three dozen used imports a month. Needless to say, Don Lucas was very happy with Bob and me.

Within two years, Don purchased a Chevrolet dealership in Los Gatos, California, and moved his operations there, taking Bob with him. Feeling I wasn't ready to take over Bob's position as general manager, Don hired an older man from the East Bay with more experience. As they say in Texas, the guy was all hat and no cattle. After three months, Bob talked Don into trusting me to run the Volvo store.

CHAPTER 5

Rise Before the Fall

*"I will make them and the places all around my hill
a blessing: and I will cause showers to come down
in their season; there shall be showers of blessing."*

Ezekiel 34:26

My ascent to running the Volvo dealership before age thirty marked a turning point in my automotive career. I helped it along with my early adaptation to something most of us take for granted today: computers. However, before my rise in the automotive business, I had to withstand a personal shock when the Hong Kong flu threatened Espe's life two months before the birth of our oldest son, Albert Basil Howell, on August 29, 1969.

A killer whose presence has almost been forgotten over time, this pandemic originated in 1968. It infected 500,000 residents in the Chinese city, about 15 percent of the population. Worldwide it caused more than a million deaths; in the U.S., it claimed approximately 33,800 lives (or almost as many American soldiers had died by that time after thirteen years of the Vietnam War). Known technically as influenza A subtype H3N2, this strain of flu was highly contagious. It was particularly bad in the San Francisco-Oakland Bay Area, which encompasses San Jose.

So, when Espe contracted a mysterious illness at the seven-month point of her pregnancy, we battled fear and uncertainty. When she checked into San Jose Hospital, she showed all the symptoms of Hong Kong flu, such as upper respiratory problems, chills, fever, and muscle pain and weakness.

She arrived in the midst of chaos. There were so many victims that soon after Espe was admitted, new arrivals were often stuck in the hallways because the hospital was filled beyond capacity. Some victims died before space came available, with panic and disorder common. It was not unusual to hear one nurse call out, "Another person just died!" and before long, a different nurse yelling, "I need a doctor with this person before she dies!"

While the symptoms of Hong Kong flu typically persisted for four to six days, Espe was hospitalized for more than a week. She spent most of her time in an oxygen tent; at one point, her temperature skyrocketed past 107 degrees. After taking a lot of medicine, she finally recovered. During her stay, she became friends with another woman suffering from the same illness. Unfortunately, that woman died.

So, two months later, when Albert came into the world as a healthy nine-pound, five-ounce child, everyone in our extended family was thrilled over baby and mother coming through this crisis unscathed. After his birth, I learned that one of the doctors at the hospital feared that Espe's bout with the flu might have impacted Albert in the womb. That it didn't is still a source of great joy.

Making History

Once the threat had passed, I turned my attention to my responsibilities at the Volvo dealership. I didn't realize it at the time, but I was living through nation-shaking history. Not only had my wife and oldest son survived the Hong Kong flu, but I would also play a small role in the advent of the personal computer in 1972 for business.

First came a brush with fame. One day, I was sitting at my desk in a small office just off the showroom. There, I could look out to the other side of the showroom and the office Don Lucas used when he came in from his dealership in Los Gatos. Suddenly, I noticed a bearded man carrying a briefcase coming out of Don's office. As I came out of my office to go outside, Don also emerged from his office.

"Who was that gentleman?" I asked.

"A guy who wants me to invest in his startup computer company," he replied. "His name is Steve Wozniak."

Yes, *that* Steve Wozniak, a native of San Jose. A few years later, Wozniak started developing the personal computer that launched Apple Computer when he and Steve Jobs began marketing it. Then in 1977, Wozniak became the primary designer of the Apple II, one of the first highly successful, mass-marketed microcomputers. Later, he also had a major influence in the initial development of the Macintosh computer before Jobs took over the project during Wozniak's absence from Apple following a major accident.

Not long after this fleeting encounter, Don told me about meeting a guy from Wang Laboratories at a Rotary Club luncheon. The man wanted to build a computer designed specifically for the automotive business. Since every dealership I had ever worked for made sales contracts by hand, I jumped at the chance to get on the cutting edge of this developing technology. Over several decades, progress saw computers reduced from a warehouse-sized operation requiring a huge cooling apparatus to keep them from melting down to something that fits in the palm of your hand. Think smartphone.

That's not to say this was a seamless transition. Despite my eagerness to switch to computers, I needed help with a new financing reality: the advent of automotive leasing. Right before our computers were finished, I called an agent for Wang to ask for help formatting a sales contract and lease agreement. Once the computer was done, we would be able to input a customer's information and forward it to the finance department.

The agent wanted to meet three days a week for three-hour sessions, for six to eight weeks, to show me the particulars. We agreed on mornings when business was usually slow, and I had backup sales agents available to handle prospects. After these grueling sessions, I told any customers who might be waiting to see me that I felt like my brain had been picked clean. I said I needed to go to lunch and eat and not talk or think for a while.

On the Move

About the same time, in December of 1972, Alameda Bank in the East Bay signed a contract with us to become a test site for their new automotive leasing contracts. The other two car dealers involved were Mercedes-Benz and Porsche dealerships. Talk about a Christmas miracle. Not only were we chosen as a test site for a computerized breakthrough alongside a pair of prestigious dealers, but I also had a legitimate lease to put on my new computer. If you think I was excited, you would be hitting the nail on the head!

So, within thirty days, I had both a new computer designed for automotive dealers and a car leasing product. Capitalizing on my technological advantage, I began airing spots on the biggest news channel radio station in Santa Clara County. We advertised a bona fide lease on a brand-new Volvo for ninety-nine dollars down and ninety-nine dollars a month for thirty-six months. (If you can do the math, that's less than $3,800, which shows you how much costs have mushroomed over the years.) Added to that was another ninety-nine dollars at signing, plus taxes and licensing fees. This offer caught considerable attention; our sales of new Volvos doubled, to between seventy-five and eighty-five per month.

"Wild West Cowboy"

Espe, Carmen, David, Billy, Emma, and me

Buzz and I met in 1968 when I was manager for a new car dealership. One day in walked this tall, handsome guy looking for a job selling cars. Because of Buzz's smooth manner, gift of gab, and sales experience, I hired him on the spot.

Back in those days, car salesmen were kind of like cowboys out of an old Wild West movie. They could walk down the street with a pair of six-shooters drawn and fire at anything in sight. In other words, a pretty loose collection of characters. The one thing they had in common was their realization that they didn't have it together. So, they tended to work hard and then party hard.

Once on board, Buzz and I hit it off immediately. Two years later, when another dealership gave me a job, I called Buzz and offered him a position as my assistant manager. Even though Buzz moved to a different dealership four years later, we stayed in touch and maintained our friendship.

However, after going through some hard times, I met Jesus. By then, Buzz lived elsewhere, but occasionally I would make a point of driving up to see him and tell him about Jesus. He'd listen politely for a while before waving bye as he called, "see you later. I have to go to lunch."

I never dreamed he would later change so dramatically.

—*Bob Rausch, longtime friend*

I also convinced Don to sponsor a sales contest for our dealership since December was normally our worst month of the year. He reluctantly agreed, but to win a Christmas trip to the Bahamas, our staff would have to sell the same number of vehicles as the previous December—in only three weeks. Sounds impossible? We did twice that number, and everyone had a ball in the islands. Throughout the next year, all the wives stayed on their husbands all year to keep selling cars; they got used to the extra money and hoped to take a return trip to the Bahamas. This positive attitude made it easier to keep everyone motivated. It also helped make Autocar Europe Volvo the number one selling Volvo dealership in twelve western states the entire time I worked there.

However, my career path would change again in 1974. At the end of 1973, Don Lucas sold the Volvo franchise to the local Mercedes dealer. In its place, Don brought in a new product to the dealership from Japan: Honda. These new-fangled cars looked so small to me, I commented, "this vehicle will never make it in the United States." I sure had to eat those words!

After only three months of selling Hondas, I moved on to San Francisco after Don bought a slow-paced Cadillac dealership in the Stonestown Galleria shopping center. On April Fool's Day, Don—along with salesmen Larry Newman, Clem Clemmensen, and me—headed up the freeway in his Cadillac to take over this dealership. It was located about seven miles from downtown, close to Lake Merced on the border of Daly City. As at Volvo, I would be the general manager. One of my first duties: to determine if any of the existing managers were capable of retaining their jobs.

Dealing in Caddies

We were all excited. At that time, Cadillac still represented the cream of the automotive industry, even though it was during a stiff challenge. The year before, the nation had endured its first gas crisis when the Organization of Petroleum Exporting Countries (OPEC) slapped an embargo on oil shipments. That caused the price of a barrel of oil to quadruple in a year, which depressed sales of gas-guzzling cars like Cadillac's.

However, since he believed this was only a temporary situation, Don saw opportunity where others saw only crisis. He was convinced the gas problems would end soon, meaning an excellent investment when things turned around. This dealership had only sold seven or eight new Cadillacs a month during the gas crisis. They still had a great sales staff of six people left; adding Larry and Clem proved to be a great fit.

When I counted the inventory of new vehicles, it came to 120. Amazingly, 70 percent of them were a shade of green, the most unpopular color for Cadillacs. That made it easy to bid the old general manager goodbye. As for turning things around, guess what idea I had that no other automotive dealers were offering then? How about ninety-nine dollars down and ninety-nine dollars a month, plus license and fees, to lease a new Cadillac?

The all-news radio station we used at that time was the biggest in the Bay Area. We promoted the small down payment and monthly lease figures in our radio ads, which brought in customers in droves. Meanwhile, I also relieved the new car manager of his duties since he had never heard of automotive leases (which became up to 75 percent of our business) and wasn't capable of arranging them.

Along with my guidance, I put Larry Newman in his place. One of the first things we did was to trade away a lot of those green Cadillacs for more popular white, silver, burgundy, and gold shades. When I asked the sales staff why there had been so many green vehicles on the lot, they said the old general manager was Irish, and that was his favorite color. Fortunately, other dealers liked Larry so much we had no problem trading away most of our green inventory.

In our first month, we sold or leased thirty-five new Cadillacs. I could see we would run out of new cars before GM shipped the 1975 models. I called the Cadillac zone office to ask about acquiring some more 1974 versions. They gave me the number of the plant that built them. When I talked to the head of the department about my problem, he said no one had called for new Cadillacs in months. The build-out for '74s was almost over; they were a week or two out from switching to 1975 Caddies.

I asked if he could help me out. He said he had eighty left, and I could order what I wanted. I said, "I'll take them." I had the confidence we could go up to forty to forty-five sales of new cars per month until the 1975s arrived. Until the next gas crisis in 1979, we would become the number one dealer in new vehicle sales in the Cadillac zone, which spanned the Bay Area and all of Northern California.

More Changes

The next area needing change was the used car department, about ten miles away in South San Francisco. The problem: a weak manager who relied on trade-ins instead of developing the skills to go out, spot quality vehicles, and acquire them for our lot. The only man I knew that I thought could help us was John Matthews. He ran the used car department at St. Claire Cadillac in San Jose and had a great industry reputation. I contacted Don Lucas, and he set up a meeting in a San Jose restaurant so we could drive down to meet John and his wife.

One of the things I admired about Don is the way he talked and interacted with people. He could laugh, kid around, compliment, and easily make friends. It was tough to persuade John to make the long drive to South San Francisco until Don said, "what if I make you a partner in the used car lot?" Naturally, that brought an enthusiastic "yes." I wasn't too upset because, at the same time, Don gave me the opportunity to purchase up to 15 percent of the new car dealership, which I was able to do three years later.

When John came aboard, he did a fantastic job. He was used to St. Claire Cadillac's big lot and major sales, but he adjusted quickly to the rhythm and flow of a smaller lot. He also hired two old-time used car professionals, who did a great job as well.

Don Lucas Cadillac was next to the parking area for a men's clothing store, flanked by a shopping mall anchored by Macy's. Across the street was a commercial building. Below ground was our service department and parts operation, as well as our business department. Our managers were great employees and really helped our bottom line.

Since the showroom had only enough room for five vehicles, we stored most of our new car inventory two miles away in a facility by Lake Merced. To avoid constantly making that trip, we parked another dozen new Caddies on the back lot. John suggested placing some one-and two-year-old Caddies in the back too. That turned out to be a great idea. If we couldn't agree with someone on a price point or lower their monthly payments enough, we could go out the back door and show them something they could afford.

With business in general improving, our dealership ran on all cylinders. We were showing a profit in every department. Some years saw a million dollars landing on our bottom line. From 1975 to 1978, we were the number one volume dealer in the Northern California Cadillac sales zone. Our best all-around year was 1978 when we sold more than 1,100 new Cadillacs.

Changes at Home

This booming business brought dramatic changes on the home front. Driving the long distance from the south end of San Jose to the dealership in San Francisco and back every day proved to be too much. I told Espe we had to sell the home so I could reduce my commute time. She agreed because I was getting home so late at night. Her parents didn't mind moving, either. We listed the house with a Realtor. Just after the sign went up, a woman knocked on the front door and asked if we had sold the home. When Espe replied we had just put up the sign, she said, "A loaded moving truck is on the way to San Jose, and we need a place to live. I will pay your asking price for your home."

We shook hands and quickly found a nice home just south of San Francisco in Burlingame. Built on the side of a mountain, it overlooked San Francisco Bay and the San Francisco International Airport. The relocation would mean a one-way commute of about fifteen miles instead of fifty-five. We moved into our new home a few days after closing.

At our home in San Jose, we had hosted many social occasions, from parties with friends to family birthdays and days where we just hung out around the swimming pool. One time we had a wedding on our front patio, complete with an arch for arriving family members and the wedding party. We continued this practice in Burlingame, even though the only way to put in a swimming pool was to dig into the side of the mountain. The pool was three feet higher at the deep end, with plenty of room to walk around. That made it easier to accommodate the mariachi bands, singers, and musicians we often invited to parties. Our neighbor put a gate on his side so people could easily go from yard to yard too.

Not long after moving, we welcomed our third child—born Donald Michael Howell (who later changed his first name to Gavin)—into the world on December 1, 1974. At twelve pounds, fifteen ounces, he was the largest baby ever delivered in San Jose's Good Samaritan Hospital. After the pool was completed, we had the first party to celebrate Donny's baptism at Our Lady of Angels Church. A festive crowd of friends and family joined us at our home.

"It's a Boy"

When I was pregnant with Donny, whom we named after Don Lucas, we lived just south of San Francisco, in Burlingame. That meant a fifty-mile trip each way to my doctor's office in San Jose. Either my mother or Buzz joined me for my visits to Dr. Scott, who had delivered our first two children at San Jose Hospital.

I trusted the doctor and felt very comfortable with him—plus, I wanted all my children to be born in the familiar environment of San Jose. At the six-month point, I struggled to climb to my feet, let alone walk. Many people asked if I was ready to deliver, but I replied, "no, I still have three months to go."

Despite this handicap, Buzz and I still went out for dinner in San Francisco. I enjoyed scenic drives down Lombard Street and always loved crossing the Golden Gate Bridge to Sausalito and Tiburon.

When D-day arrived on December 1, 1974, we drove to San Jose Hospital with Charlene in the back seat, listening to "Having My Baby" by Paul Anka—over and over. After we arrived around 2:00 p.m., they rushed me into the operating room for a C-section. Our youngest son weighed twelve pounds and fifteen ounces, a new hospital record. It stood for twelve years.

Many people crowded into my room afterward and brought flowers. Among those posing questions was a reporter from the San Jose Mercury News, which ran a story about the birth in the next day's paper. to the festive flavor of the occasion, my sister had her daughter, Rosie, the dayafter I gave birth and joined me in the samehospital room.

Meanwhile, no matter who was there, Buzz stood in the room and proudly smiled from ear to ear as he handed out cigars with "It's a Boy" on the wrapper.

—*Espe Howell, Wife*

We lived in Burlingame for three years until we had the chance to buy an acre of land in Hillsborough, a few miles to the west. There we would move into a spacious new home designed by Espe's uncle, architect Clemente Troncoso and built by Larry Newman's father, Howard. However, we had an interim period to endure after selling our house in Burlingame. We had used the net proceeds to buy the new property and establish a line of equity at Bank of America to draw on for construction costs. Since the house required more than six months to build, we had to rent a home nearby.

Summer Vacation

Our years in the San Francisco area were delightful family times. We had many visits before Halloween to the pumpkin patches in Half Moon Bay and downtown San Francisco to enjoy all the Christmas lights, decorations, and festive atmosphere for the holiday season.

Many summers, we went to Lakeport, a small town about three hours to the north on the west shore of Clear Lake. In the summer, we used our boat for water skiing. Charlene and Albert became very proficient at the sport and couldn't wait to go skiing, especially over holiday weekends. The best thing about working in San Francisco in the automotive business was the workforce was unionized, so during the week, the lot closed promptly at 6:00 p.m. and didn't open on Sunday. As general manager, I made up a schedule for Larry Newman, John Matthews, and myself that allowed each of us to take every third weekend off—Friday through Sunday. All three families used our boat for skiing. When our turn came, we always loved the three days of water skiing.

At the time, I was also coaching Albert's Little League team. Frankly, I did a pretty poor job of selecting talent during the draft. That meant our team lost a lot of games, so after practice, I would have the whole team running bases as punishment. When our team finally won a game, one of the kids yelled out, "can we stop running after practice?" I replied, "I'm buying everyone ice cream after the game."

As I look back at those summer breaks, I appreciate a man like Chuck giving me a hard time, which forced me to work harder and prove myself. My work ethic earned his respect. One time, about seven years after I worked for him, he was nice enough to invite our family on an outing to Lakeport after another couple had to cancel their plans. Of all our vacations, the best were spent skiing around twenty-five-mile-long Clear Lake. Those were such joyful times; even the anticipation during the drive to the motel in Lakeport, where we usually stayed, felt exhilarating. Lakeport had a great small-town feel, and the motel sat near the water, separated from it by only a lush green lawn.

In addition to fun family outings, after moving to Burlingame, we joined a group of couples who would dine out once a month. The couple was serving as hosts that month would pick the restaurant. We would meet at their home for a drink and a few snacks before going to dinner. Most people were our age and newcomers to the area.

Whenever we had friends or family members in from out of town, we usually went to San Francisco to see the sights. Our favorites were Fisherman's Wharf and nearby Pier 39, a waterfront complex with numerous restaurants, shops, and other attractions. Pier 39 had a fantastic view of the Golden Gate Bridge, which we liked to drive over into Marin County. Interestingly, it didn't cost anything to leave, but we had to pay several dollars (by 2020, it had risen to seven) to cross the bridge back into San Francisco. We also would take visitors riding on the cable cars and to see Chinatown, the Palace of Fine Arts, Nob Hill, and the Palace Hotel.

The Palace Hotel's Garden Court featured an incredible Sunday brunch. Not only was the food great, but it's an elegant, majestic place. Its ornate chandeliers, glass dome, and iconic marble columns transported you back to the 1920s. Indeed, the city's restaurants were one of the prime attractions for our guests. While we loved taking day trips around San Francisco and Marin County, a visit to one of the countless great restaurants put the icing on the cake, so to speak. We usually recommended the Sears Family Restaurant on Powell Street for breakfast, the seafood at Scoma's on Fisherman's Wharf for lunch, and any number of places for dinner.

Beginning of the End

Soon after I became a 15 percent partner in Don Lucas Cadillac, we took a vacation to Kauai—sometimes called the "Garden Island"—in Hawaii. We went to visit Espe's Aunt Lupe and Uncle Herbert. They showed us all around the island, the fourth-largest and northern-most in the series of islands that make up Hawaii. We had a great time!

One day at the beach, Espe was feeling rejected. Instead of paying any attention to her, I got engrossed in a politically oriented conversation with two other men. We were chatting about Ronald Reagan, who had finished his second term as California's governor in 1975. I commented about how I thought Reagan was a great governor and would make an excellent president if he ran (and I felt he proved me right during the 1980s).

Despite the slight irritation my behavior caused Espe that day, our trip was largely a success. Kauai's combination of tropical rain forests, picturesque waterfalls, mountain peaks, and meandering rivers would fit most people's definition of paradise. With its largest town of only around ten thousand people, the island has a truly laid-back atmosphere. Like the Hawaiians often say: "No worries, brothers."

However, not too many months after our vacation, I received a rude awakening: the end to my time at Don Lucas Cadillac. It stemmed from the 1979 energy crisis, the decade's second oil-price shock. This one stemmed from decreased oil output in the wake of the revolution that replaced the Shah of Iran with the first of a series of ayatollahs to act as the nation's supreme ruler. Ironically, although global supplies only declined by 4 percent, widespread panic drove prices much higher. The price of crude oil more than doubled in a year. In the first energy crisis in 1973-1974, it had been common to see long lines of motorists waiting to fuel up their cars. Now, they reappeared.

Because of these conditions, several states passed mandatory gasoline rationing, including California, New York, Pennsylvania, Texas, and New Jersey. Consumers could only purchase gas every other day, based on whether the last digit of their license plate ended in an even or odd number. While I wanted to fight and not give in to the spreading panic, Don ordered me to cut all advertising, the first of several cost-cutting measures. As I feared, this reduced our sales to ten or fifteen vehicles a month. We sank from number one in sales to seventh in the Cadillac zone.

As you can imagine, my pride plunged along with our sales numbers. The last straw proved to be a meeting where I met the region's top dealer from Hayward, located in the East Bay about twenty miles south of Oakland. I asked the guy how they were doing so well in a horrible automobile market. He replied, "I'm doing exactly what you used to do, including ninety-nine dollars down and ninety-nine-dollars-a-month lease payments. On the same radio station you used to advertise on."

Talk about a low blow! I left that meeting feeling so sad. If we hadn't stopped advertising, our business might have gone down some, but nowhere near as badly. That day, my pride got the best of me, prompting me to call a friend who was the general manager at a Cadillac dealership in Oakland. Knowing he wanted to leave his job, I said, "I'm leaving here if you're interested in taking over."

"Absolutely," he replied.

The next day, I went to see Don to hand in my resignation.

"Are you sure?" he said.

"Yes."

Just like that, my friend from Oakland had replaced me. There I was, out the door and with no idea of where to go next. What I didn't know at the time was that I was on the cusp of making the biggest and most earth-shaking decision of my life.

CHAPTER 6

Finding Pure Water

On the last day, that great day of the feast, Jesus stood and cried out, saying, "If anyone thirsts, let him come to Me and drink. He who believes in Me, as the Scripture has said, out of his heart will flow rivers of living water."

John 7:37-38

"I, Jesus, have sent My angel to testify to you these things in the churches. I am the Root and the Off-spring of David, the Bright and Morning Star." And the Spirit and the bride say, "Come!" And let him who hears say, "Come!" And let him who thirsts come. Whoever desires, let him take the water of life freely.

Revelation 22:16-17

Looking back, I can see how foolish I was to leave Don Lucas Cadillac with no idea of where to go next. Bailing water, I did the only thing I could think of: call folks I knew in the automotive business to see if they had any leads. Fortunately, one told me about the new owners of St. Claire Cadillac in Santa Clara looking for managers. So, I called and made an appointment with Joe Balestra, a minority partner with Mervin Morris, who had just sold all fifty of his Mervyn's department stores in three states. (Morris had opened his first store in San Lorenzo in 1949 and over three decades prospered to the point the chain was acquired by Dayton Hudson Corporation, the forerunner to Target. The number of stores nearly quadrupled after Dayton Hudson acquired it and retained it as a separate division, although Mervyn's ultimately filed for bankruptcy in 2008.)

Joe and I hit it off immediately. When I had worked at All-American Pontiac in San Jose, I used to visit Joe's Pontiac store in nearby Redwood City and buy some used cars from his used car manager. It turned out St. Claire Cadillac had already hired a general manager from a Mercedes-Benz store who was friends with Morris. The new general manager was bringing a new car manager with him, but Joe told me the used car manager's job was open. Although becoming a used car manager after running the show for two dealerships might seem like a backward move, I saw it as a great opportunity. Hunger can do that for you. Or, as Proverbs 16:18 puts it, "Pride goes before destruction, and a haughty spirit before a fall."

Even though the latest energy crisis hadn't ended by November of 1979, there was still a good market for used cars. The used car lot had room for 100 to 120 automobiles, but there were less than forty there. Wanting to bring in some additional inventory, I decided to head several hundred miles south to Los Angeles to buy some used vehicles. At my first auto auction on a Tuesday morning, I bought more than a dozen cars. The next day in Anaheim, I bought nearly a dozen more, a pattern I repeated for the next few weeks.

Meanwhile, once we started advertising, the energy crisis subsided, and our salesmen started making deals; we saw a booming business. The new car department was doing well too, thanks to Morris running full-page ads in the San Jose Mercury News. All this activity resulted in the dealership advancing to the number one position in the Northern California Cadillac zone.

Change of Direction

Meanwhile, even though it made little immediate impact on me, in the summer of 1978, Espe made a decision to follow Jesus Christ as her Lord and Savior. Although she had spent her whole life in the Catholic church, she never knew that she could have a personal relationship with Him. Knowing the Lord as an active, alive, and calming presence in her daily life instead of a Sunday-only God who she forgot about the rest of the week made all the difference in the world.

Espe's encounter with the Holy Spirit took place during the peak of a significant spiritual movement known in Christian circles as the charismatic renewal. This powerful move of the Holy Spirit touched numerous denominations and prompted the formation of many charismatic and Pentecostal churches. It also fueled the growth of Full Gospel Business Men's Fellowship International (FGBFMI), a lay-led organization founded by Demos Shakarian, a dairy farmer from Downey, California. Though its origins were in the US, it gradually expanded worldwide, and I would later serve as president of its San Jose chapter.

"Spiritual Awakening"

A decade into our marriage, our relationship was fraying at the edges. Buzz liked going out Friday nights with his friends to hit the bars in San Francisco. I stewed about that—and a lot of other things.

At the time, the charismatic movement was sweeping across the nation. As a result,

the Catholic church in San Jose, my mother attended, started hosting special services in a school gymnasium on Friday nights. One Friday night while Buzz was out, my mother asked if I would like to join her while my father stayed home with the kids. After much mental debate, I decided to go.

When we arrived, we struggled to find a parking space since more than eight hundred people had flocked to the meeting. When we walked in, it felt really strange. The singing, exuberant praise, and dancing—we never did those things in church! Everyone had a Bible, and they were all so happy! When the music ended, people walked up to share their testimony.

After his sermon, Father Bush asked us to divide into groups of five to pray for each other. In our group, a woman placed her hand on another woman's shoulder as a man said softly, "Jesus, come into her heart. She wants You."

"Yes, Jesus, once You go into her heart, I want You in mine," I thought.

Wham! Instantly I fell backward. Somebody caught me, but I wasn't alarmed. I felt like I was floating on a cloud. Suddenly, I felt like something heavy leave my heart—all the bitterness, resentment, and hatred that had gradually built up against my husband. I burst into tears when the pressure left my chest. It felt amazing.

After about twenty minutes, a man helped me to my feet and handed me a gospel tract titled "Born Again." I laughed and put the tract in my pocket. I was the happiest person on earth, although I had no idea how that had happened; In a word: incredible.

—*Espe Howell, Wife*

FBGMFI played a role in many Catholics receiving the gift of the Holy Spirit and sometimes featured Catholic priests as speakers at some of its meetings. Ironically, a Catholic priest named Father Bush led the service where Espe would pray to receive Christ as her Savior. It was held in a meeting hall next to the Catholic church in Santa Clara. At the end of that service, Father Bush asked everyone to split into groups of five and pray for each other. Espe, her mother, a friend, and two strangers gathered in a circle to do that.

As one of the women prayed and declared that she believed in Jesus as Lord and Savior, Espe thought to herself: "Okay, after her, You can come into my heart too." Before she could put those thoughts into a verbal prayer, Espe sensed a spiritual wave overwhelming her. As she fell backward, someone caught her and laid her gently on the floor. There, Espe felt great joy, love, and peace flooding her heart. The anger, resentment, and bitterness that had been gradually building in her heart toward me during twelve years of marriage floated away.

When Espe and her mother returned home, I noticed something very different about Espe. It was as if she glowed. When I asked her where they had been, she calmly explained what had happened. But that was like talking to a brick wall. After listening to her story, instead of being amazed, I shrugged it off as some kind of "religious experience" and gave it little thought.

Little did I know what a powerful move had touched my wife. The meetings that Father Bush had been leading were a result of a wave of revival among Catholic priests that had started in the eastern part of the US. At the same time, a coinciding emphasis on the power of the Holy Spirit (which overcame Espe during that prayer circle) created a hunger for more of God and His power inside and outside of the Catholic church. Ultimately, it led many priests—including Father Bush—to leave Catholicism behind.

Soon after Espe's profound experience with the Spirit, she got angry at me one day for failing to pay attention to her. Just then, a stranger approached and asked Espe if she was a Christian. When Espe nodded, the woman replied she had a message from God: "Open your Bible to 1 Peter 3:1-2 (NIV). When Espe did, she read:

> Wives, in the same way submit yourselves to your own husbands so that, if any of them do not believe the word, they may be won over without words by the behavior of their wives, when they see the purity and reverence of your lives.

With this Scripture in mind, my wife started going into our bedroom closet and praying regularly for me, saying, "Lord, give Basil no peace, comfort, joy, or rest in this world until he makes Jesus Christ Lord of his life." Everywhere she went, she repeated this prayer whenever she had the time—around fifty times a day. Following the advice of 1 Peter 3:1-2, she transformed her conduct too. Instead of snarling at me or picking fights, she smiled a lot and said nice things while cooking great dinners. She also left her Bible around our house so I would see it, hoping I would understand this Book was responsible for her becoming a sweeter, better, nicer wife.

"Miracle of Rebirth"

The night I accepted Christ as my Savior and Lord, I tried to explain what happened to my mother. She didn't understand—it would be more than thirty years before she made the same decision in her heart. But I didn't mind. No one could take away the peace I felt.

Once we returned home, I sat on the chair in our bedroom, blinking my eyes and trying to decide how I would explain the amazing things that had happened to my husband. When Buzz came home from cruising the bars, he expected an argument over him being out late again.

"I'm tired and need to get sleep," he said with a sigh. "Let's get it over with."

Because of the joy pulsating in my heart, I just smiled. Still obviously elated, he asked where I had gone that night. Moving over to the edge of the bed, I told him where we had been, handed him the gospel tract, and explained a little bit about the meeting and how different it was from a typical church service.

Afterward, I went to another room so I could pray quietly for him. I wanted him to experience the same feelings, joy, and exhilaration. No one told me how to pray or how it should go, but the Holy Spirit guided me to be able to pray for Buzz. The words that came to me were: "Heavenly Father, give Buzz no peace, no comfort, no joy, no rest in this world until he makes Jesus Christ the Lord of his life."

For fifteen months, I prayed for Buzz to find the Lord. Then the miracle happened. We have been joint heirs and fellow laborers for Christ ever since.

—*Espe Howell, Wife*

Answered Prayer

Whoever thinks prayer doesn't work has never been the topic of my wife's faithful intercession. Soon after Espe started praying for me, I found myself engaged in strange behavior. Every time I left the dealership after work and headed to a bar, I would get tongue-tied when I tried to strike up a conversation with other people (especially women). This was before the booze even had a chance to take effect. What's more, I would go home feeling soberer than before entering the bar. In addition to my fits with getting tongue-tied, I regularly ran into friends or acquaintances who would ask me: "Why don't you go home to your wife?"

In the midst of these puzzling experiences, I hopped on an airplane to Southern California. Bound for an automotive auction in Rosemead, just east of Los Angeles, I planned to add to the used car inventory at St. Claire Cadillac. I had a good day, buying enough vehicles to load up two large car carriers.

Early that afternoon, I met up with a friend who was buying used Mercedes-Benz autos in Beverly Hills. After enjoying lunch at a nice restaurant, I tried to keep up drinking Scotch and waters with an Australian guy who grew up winning drinking contests. He literally drank me under the table. After drinking all afternoon, I called another friend in the area, who suggested we meet for dinner in the seaside mecca of Marina del Rey. Naturally, I did some more drinking, to the point I was ready to pass out. Which is what I did after he told me his boat was docked out behind the restaurant.

I woke up, bleary-eyed, on the boat at 7:00 a.m. the next day. After trying to rub the cobwebs out of my brain, I headed off to another auction in Anaheim with a major hangover and in no shape to buy any more vehicles. So, I grabbed a late afternoon flight out of John Wayne Airport in Orange County, landing in the San Francisco airport around 6:30 p.m. Despite my still-fuzzy brain, I asked Espe to take me to the seven o'clock Wednesday night service at Our Lady of Angels in Burlingame. The night before had been the worst night of my life, and I felt a need to get closer to God.

This was part of God's perfect timing; the priest speaking that night was Father John, who had baptized our youngest son, Donny, and spoken a blessing over our home in the foothills soon after we moved into it. That night, Father John spoke about how a husband should treat his wife and children; he should love them, cherish his wife, be a strong role model, and act as the moral leader in the home. In short, all the things I was not.

After the service, I went to confession and shared a lifetime of my darkest sins. I have no idea how long I was in confession. Remembering what Espe had told me about her salvation experience, I added: "Now I want to ask Jesus Christ to come into my heart."

I expected the priest to tell me to repeat a lot of rosary prayers, like a hundred "Our Fathers" and "Hail Marys," and perform many acts of contrition too. The priest was so taken aback by my true confession; he simply said: "Go in peace and sin no more." Believe it or not, I felt totally cleansed. The burden of sin lifted gloriously from my shoulders. I left the church feeling guilt-free, like a new man, and totally cleansed. It was the greatest experience. On the drive home, Espe said, "When you walked out of the confessional, I could see a glow all around you."

This happened the week before Christmas of 1979. What a joyous holiday that year!

Growing in Grace

That Sunday, we took our children to Our Lady of Angels. Afterward, we asked Father John if there was someplace else we could go to learn more about God. He motioned to a woman named Peggy Nugetti, who was happy and excited when she learned about the decision I had made and that both Espe and I were living for Christ now. She invited us to an evening Bible study a few days later in the church hall next to the sanctuary. When we arrived, we found a small group of people about ten to twenty years older than us. Feeling blessed just to be there, we joined in songs and Bible study the best we could. In the end, we all joined in a circle. The leader asked if anyone had a testimony to share.

I lifted my hand and told everyone what happened during my time of confession the previous week. They all started jumping and rejoicing. Soon, someone asked if I wanted to be baptized in the Holy Spirit. I replied, "if it is from God, I want to receive it." Everyone laid their hands on me and started praying for the gift of the Holy Spirit to manifest itself in me, with power. In a few minutes, I was speaking in a language I didn't recognize. The leader said, "that's God's heavenly voice." It's as 2 Corinthians 5:17 puts it: "Therefore, if anyone is in Christ, he is a new creation; old things have passed away; behold, all things have become new."

When we returned to this Bible study the following week, we again joined in a circle for prayer after the singing and Bible study. As various people took turns praying, someone said, "God is calling someone to open their home for Bible study and God's work." I turned to Espe and said, "that's us." By February, Espe had sent out flyers and made phone calls to numerous friends and neighbors around Hillsborough and Burlingame, inviting them to a Friday night Bible study at our house. Such home-based groups were common across the nation during the 1960s, 1970s, and 1980s, with all kinds of reports of answered prayers, healings, and miracles circulating throughout churches and FGBMFI meetings.

Twelve people attended that first meeting; within six months, the turnouts had surpassed forty. One of the people at the first meeting was a pastor from San Mateo named Gil Mandigo. He soon started preaching at the meetings, with his wife playing piano in magnificent fashion. We also witnessed people praying and making decisions to follow Christ, lives dramatically changed for the better to God's Glory and miracles of healing. One example: our youngest son had a severe earache and high temperature, but he was healed instantly after our group prayed for him.

We didn't see such miracles take place until after we heard that word about God wanting someone to open their home for His work. We had no clue of how this was happening, but two nuns who traveled around the US in their motor home had a unique spin on things. Espe met them at the Wednesday night Bible study at Our Lady of Angels. Two nights later, the nuns attended the meeting at our home.

After they sang beautifully, Pastor Gil gave a great message about Jesus, His tremendous love for us by going to the cross for our sins, His blood bringing forth the new life, and how Jesus is the only way to heaven. That night our daughter, Charlene, and her friend—who had both just turned thirteen—accepted Jesus as their Savior. (Forty years later, Charlene still loves Jesus.) That night, a friend named Irma Taptia also came to Christ. What a fantastic night of celebration!

Word of the miraculous healings, conversions, and personal breakthroughs started to circulate through our neighborhood and well beyond. Some nights the crowd swelled to fifty or more. Not necessarily front-page news or something that would excite the world, but those who came were blessed mightily. I get giddy now just thinking about this welcome to the reality of a walk with Christ.

"Wisdom of a Young Man"

I was just a small "chico" when I met Basil Howell in 1966 while he was courting my big sister. I'll never forget when they started dating, and my parents sent me along as a chaperone. It was the start of a wonderful, lifelong relationship.

After this courtship flourished into marriage, Basil and Espe moved to Northern California. As their family grew, they needed more room, and my father helped them buy their second home. In return, Basil and Espe welcomed my parents, sister, and me into their household.

While we were essentially one big happy family, through the years, we experienced the kind of trials and tribulations most of us go through in life. My parents, Esperanza and Alberto Jimenez were instrumental in raising and building a loving home with compassion—yet a stern hand when needed. As the oldest of thirteen children, Esperanza Senior learned this combination, helping raise her younger siblings.

For me, growing up in two affluent areas just south of San Francisco was a blessing and a learning experience. One evening I attended a teenage Bible study, where I met the Holy Spirit and accepted Jesus as my personal Lord and Savior. When I got home, I was so joyful that Basil, Espe, and my parents thought I was high or drunk, but I was drunk on the pure Holy Spirit. Soon the Lord also started working on Basil and Espe. After some personal trials, they made the same decision I did. So did my parents as they neared the end of their lives.

I am thankful for the ways my upbringing and the large extended family in which I grew up enriched my life. God is good.

—*Brother-in-law Edward Jimenez*

Importance of Worship

The major lesson we learned the night our daughter decided to follow Jesus was the crucial importance of worship to any Christian meeting or service. In fact, it's more than just singing. It's creating a true relationship with our Savior, who gave up His life on the cross for all sins now, past, and future. Worship should be with all our hearts, soul, and innermost being. As John 4:24 teaches: "God is Spirit, and those who worship Him must worship in spirit and truth."

We also learned about the central importance of the Bible and how it needed to be more than a Sunday showpiece or a coffee table book. So many of us were spiritual infants that we had to learn how to go from the Old Testament to the New Testament. On a practical basis, we also learned the importance of starting on time, arranging the songs and music for worship, finding a gifted person to lead the meetings, and having the right person to teach the Word. With Pastor Gil, we had the latter covered. One outstanding quality I remember about Gil was his patience and love to help new believers—especially Espe and me—start our walk with Christ on the right path.

In addition to Pastor Gil's leadership, we had help setting up every Friday night from faithful friends like Peggy Nugetti and Carmen Lutrel. They had become great friends of ours and also invited us to join them at different Christian events in the Bay Area. We enjoyed Christian fellowship at various lunches and dinners at each other's homes too. They always demonstrated unconditional love for us and others, especially during times of prayer at the end of Friday night meetings. They had so much faith that many people received healing or saw other prayers answered, whether a need on their job, a rebellious child or a vexing personal situation.

One of the highlights from those early meetings was the night a singer named Noel McFarland visited. I felt like his voice was a gift from heaven; the anointing that obviously rested on his singing was truly a gift for everyone who attended the meeting. It helped create a spirit of joy and worship that felt like being bathed in a precious, pure oil—something better experienced in person than described in words. After the message, Noel returned with some records and other mementos. People there snapped up everything he brought.

Finding a Church Home

God is so good. In fact, He has great plans for His people that include using others in our lives to bless us. Case in point: Bob and Karen Rausch, who originally invited us to visit Crossroads Bible Church in San Jose. We loved the worship and the anointed preaching and teaching of Pastor Rich Marshall. (Later, God led Pastor Rich and his wife, Wilma, to leave church ministry to speak, teach, and write about the budding market-place ministry movement. He has also written three books, with his debut, God @Work, selling more than fifty thousand copies. In more recent times, he has been hosting a television program of the same name on GodTV).

Visiting Crossroads Bible ended up being a great move for us. Soon after we started attending, Pastor Rich began an expository, line-by-line, book-by-book exploration of the Bible. It took about five and a half years for him to cover Genesis (the first book) to Revelation (the last book). Not only did we like the biblically-based preaching and teaching, but our children also loved the Sunday school classes at Crossroads. During Bible study hour, Espe would attend a Spanish-speaking class with her grandmother and aunt; both came to know Christ as their Savior through my wife's influence. After those sessions, Espe would join me in the sanctuary, where we always sat in the first row facing the pulpit.

"Move of the Spirit"

It was a wonderful season at Crossroads Bible Church when Bob and Karen Rausch brought their friends Buzz and Espe Howell into our midst. Looking back, two major thoughts run through my mind. The first is that both couples' presence was an example of a powerful marketplace ministry movement.

Although I left the pulpit in 2000 to become a full-time speaker, author, and GodTV host, in the early 1980s, I had no concept of this movement. It found early expression through Full Gospel Business Men's Fellowship International, Women's Aglow, and other marketplace-oriented ministries.

Bob Rausch brought many of his car industry contacts to the Lord and to Crossroads Church. The stories that Buzz recounts in this chapter and others made a powerful impact. The fact is marketplace ministry did not originate with the work of any human. It was, and still is, the work of Almighty God, using whom He will! I am so thankful to play a small part and to hear again of its long-lasting impact.

My thoughts also went to the powerful change that came through the charismatic renewal of the 1960s, 1970s, and 1980s; bright memories came alive for my wife, Wilma, and I as we read. We knew the Word, and Buzz and Espe knew the Holy Spirit. Later,

**when we encountered the power of the Holy
Spirit firsthand in Argentina, it had a lot to
do with many of our friends, like the How-
ells, praying for us.**

**I might say it this way: underneath my
teaching, they received the Word, and later
we received the personal walk and power
gifts of the Holy Spirit. We all need both the
Word and the Spirit.**

—*Rich Marshall*
Buzz Howell's former pastor

Bob and Karen Rausch were generally in the first
row too. As mature believers, they offered tremendous
examples to Espe and me of how we should live our lives
as followers of Christ. Indeed, Bob baptized Espe, me,
and our three children at Crossroads; they were such
close friends that Pastor Rich approved our request for
Bob to handle the ceremony.

While this is tough for a formerly hard-bitten guy
like me to admit, when we first went to Crossroads, I
would cry like a baby whenever Pastor Rich spoke from
the Bible and mentioned Jesus Christ or salvation. I always had to ask for some tissues to wipe the tears from
my eyes. I usually experienced twinges of embarrass-
ment during these weeping sessions since it felt like everyone in the sanctuary could see me blubbering like a

newborn. This went on for several weeks before I finally gained enough composure to not get overly emotional all the time.

A few months after we started attending Cross-roads, a Vietnamese woman who had started an early Sunday morning service for primarily Vietnamese-speaking people approached me at the end of our second service. (At that time, thousands of Vietnamese immigrants were coming to San Jose and other communities around Northern and Southern California.)

Margaret, who had taken an American name after marrying a man from the U.S., had heard about our Friday night meetings through Bob Rausch. She thought I would be a good speaker for her service. Although a brilliant woman who could speak several languages, she was trying to lead the group by herself. Since the Vietnamese didn't respond well to female leadership, I asked if I could help. I looked at my wife, who nodded. We agreed to give it a try.

God blessed those meetings in a powerful way. I used to study Scripture intensively to prepare and make sure my messages were biblically accurate. The spiritual flow we enjoyed with Margaret was beautiful beyond description. We reached the point where when I laughed, she did too. When I got excited, so did Margaret. As a result, many Vietnamese people came to know Jesus Christ as Savior. During our time at that church, God moved in miraculous ways. Many immigrants were healed of diseases they had contracted in Vietnam and other illnesses.

Part of Vietnamese class with Margaret and us

Their exposure to the Word went beyond this service. Afterward, they followed Margaret to the balcony, where she would translate Pastor Rich's messages via headsets worn by her listeners. At times, she would translate into two or three languages, depending on who was there.

Changed Lives

Because of our involvement with the Vietnamese ministry, Espe and I received numerous invitations to birthday and holiday parties, as well as weddings. Margaret even asked me to officiate at two wedding ceremonies. The first time she asked, I told her I wasn't even sure it would be considered legal, but she replied, "they already have their city license. Besides, they consider you their pastor." What could I say? I learned how to do a marriage ceremony. Those two weddings were a sign—even a seal of approval—from God to be open to Christ's love for everything He wants to do in our lives to help others be better followers of Jesus and to bless them too.

Espe still vividly remembers the first time I preached to that class. When I finished, I said to the class (with Margaret interpreting in Vietnamese), "if anyone needs a healing, come forward." There were between forty and fifty people there that day, and each one of them came to the front. After Margret asked where they needed healing, she interpreted the information for Espe and me. I would ask the Holy Spirit to lead our intercession as we prayed for each need. God gets all the glory for the healings of many afflictions we saw that day. In addition, some surrendered their lives to Christ and asked Him to come into their hearts and live as Lord and Savior.

After the meeting, Margret told us these people had all lived in Communist concentration camps before coming to the United States. I could not imagine living in freezing weather without proper clothing and horrible conditions. Yet, in an example of God's power to change lives, half a dozen attendees—and many of their relatives—at that service saw their circumstances change dramatically. It came with the help of a wealthy Vietnamese man who backed them financially after they scraped together modest investments to open some doughnut shops.

The shop owners stopped coming on Sunday; when Margaret investigated further, we learned they had to open their shop early to take advantage of the Sunday morning crowds who loved doughnuts (a number of them on their way to church). Instead of getting angry about them missing services, we showed them how happy we were that they were able to better their lives. We encouraged them to stay involved with the congregation and to come to midweek Bible study or other events when they didn't have to mind the store.

You may remember me saying in chapter two that in some ways, the good old days weren't that good. But our experiences at Crossroads Bible were one instance where the good old days were very good.

CHAPTER 7

A Life Rescued

"For God so loved the world that He gave His only begotten Son, that whoever believes in Him should not perish but have everlasting life."

John 3:16

No sooner had we stepped out of the terminal at O'Hare Airport than I wondered, "who turned off the heat?" The air stung with the force of a championship boxer, laden with humidity and mixed with a wintry chill that made it feel like getting smacked by one of Muhammad Ali's punches. Chicago has long been known as the Windy City, but as far as I was concerned, they could call it the Windy and Freezing Colder than an Icebox City!

"If Nebraska is this cold, I'm sure glad mom took us to California," I mumbled as Bob Rausch, and I waited outside for a rental car shuttle. Fortunately, this was a few years before Chicago set several all-time lows, with temperatures ranging from a frigid twenty-three degrees below zero to its all-time low of minus twenty-seven in January of 1980.

Still, a nasty wind blew off Lake Michigan the January day Bob and I flew to Illinois, home base, for our used car acquisition trip. As distasteful as I found the subfreezing temperatures, the cold also worked to our advantage. With the onset of winter, car prices around Chicago followed the same direction as the thermometer. Bob, who worked for a Chevrolet dealer not far from St. Claire Cadillac, could pick up used Chevys and save two thousand dollars or more, compared to prices on the West Coast. At the car auctions we visited, I could find Cadillacs for three to four thousand dollars less than I would have paid in California. With transportation in those days only running about $250 per car, the savings more than paid for our airfares and other expenses.

On Tuesday, we went to an auction in Chicago before flying across Lake Michigan on Wednesday for another auction in the Detroit suburb of Dearborn. On Thursday, we returned to Chicago for another auction. Before making that first trip in early 1980, I had to prepare for the snow and cold by shopping at Mel Cotton's Outdoor Outfitters, a sporting goods store in San Jose. Its sign has the appearance of Outdoor Man, the fictional store managed by Tim Allen on the Last Man Standing comedy show.

When we went to our first auction, I dressed for the day by donning two or three shirts and sweaters, a heavy-duty down-filled jacket, and bulky cold-weather shoes that made it look like I could easily jog over to Soldier Field and kick field goals for the Chicago Bears. Yet, when we made it inside the building, eighty-degree temperatures greeted us. Naturally, within minutes, I was peeling off clothes as the cars came floating past on conveyor belts. That first day I bought nine pre-owned Cadillacs. The next day in Dearborn, I found a larger selection of beautiful Caddies, buying eighteen of them for our lot. On Thursday back in Chicago, I purchased another ten vehicles at another auction.

When we flew home, I looked up the Kelly Blue Book—the bible of automotive pricing—values. I learned that we had averaged $3,800 per car under the low-end, wholesale blue book price, meaning we sold them for a nifty profit. That winter, I made several trips back east before the market rose to normal levels in March. These deals helped jump-started our year. So did a rise in new vehicle sales after the second gas crisis ended amid a glut of oil production that year. Soon, we were seeing hundreds of customers responding to the full-page ads the dealership placed in the San Jose *Mercury News*.

Spiritual Waves

This change of fortune in the car business paralleled the spiritual boost we received from the weekly Bible studies I attended with Espe, followed by the Friday night home Bible studies we started hosting, which I mentioned in chapter six. At one of those studies, I learned what would become one of my favorite Scriptures: "But you shall receive power when the Holy Spirit has come upon you; and you shall be witnesses to Me in Jerusalem, and in all Judea and Samaria, and to the end of the earth" (Acts 1:8).

To add to the spiritual excitement fanned by these meetings, we learned that renowned evangelist Billy Graham would be coming to San Jose's Spartan Stadium on October 17, 1981. This was less than two years after I had made the decision to follow Jesus, and I was excited to be able to see Graham in person. Naturally, I invited Joe Balestra, who had become a good friend after I became the used car manager at St. Claire Cadillac. When the time came, my wife and I picked up Joe and his girlfriend in nearby Menlo Park, arriving early to get some good seats. As we watched, thousands of people streamed into the stadium.

"A Changed Man"

I knew God had seriously touched Buzz's heart the day I saw him at a car auction, and we wound up talking for two hours about Jesus. Buzz had been under conviction; the Holy Spirit had been talking to him about his need for a Savior. While he traces his conversion to a confessional session with a Catholic priest, I believe this day marked a new spiritual awareness for him. Sitting in a hot car, he affirmed that Jesus is Lord.

Not long after our chat, Buzz and Espe drove forty miles to sit with my wife and me in the front row at Crossroads Bible Church in San Jose. What I remember most about Buzz was his Kleenex. He couldn't sit through a sermon about Jesus without sobbing and reaching for a tissue.

One thing Buzz and I have had in common for many years is a love of telling people about Jesus. Consequently, we wound up with a pew at Crossroads, getting nicknamed "Car Row." We called it that because so many coworkers and associates from the car business came to hear about Christ.

One thing led to another, and Buzz and Espe felt God leading them to open their home for a "come-one, come-all" prayer and praise meeting. Upwards of seventy-five people would show up on any given Friday night.

One memorable occasion happened when a guy got slain in the Spirit. After he fell down in a heap and Buzz leaned over to pick him up, the back of Buzz's pants split right down the middle! With a loud booming sound, I might add.

I could tell of many instances of God working in our lives together. But in conclusion, I want to say this that to know Buzz and Esperanza is to love them. That's what's most important. I especially love how God—the Master and Maker of all—brought us together before we knew Jesus and then made us brothers through His blood, shed on the cross.

—*Bob Rausch, longtime friend*

The Billy Graham Evangelistic Association always invited many local church choirs and musical teams to sing and play together at his crusades. When they sang and played great worship music, the audience stood and sang in one accord. (Today, as I look back to my visit to heaven and think about the music and worship, what I felt at Graham's meeting was very close to the feelings I enjoyed in heaven.) After the choirs finished, noted soloist George Beverly Shay came onstage and gave a magnificent performance of old gospel songs.

Finally, Graham came to the podium and delivered a great sermon on the "five Ws" of Christ's second coming. The five Ws, which I discovered online thirty-eight years after hearing them in person, include:

1. **Watch:** Matthew 16:3: "And in the morning, 'It will be foul weather today, for the sky is red and threatening.' Hypocrites! You know how to discern the face of the sky, but you cannot discern the signs of the times." Graham warned his listeners to watch for signs among the day's current events.

2. **Wait:** Hebrews 10:37: "For yet a little while and he who is coming will come and will not tarry." Along this line, Graham also quoted Habakkuk 2:3: "For the vision is yet for an appointed time; but at the end it will speak, and it will not lie. Though it tarries, wait for it; because it will surely come, it will not tarry."

3. **Walk:** To serve God, He wants us to walk faithfully as His disciples, living godly lives.

4. Work: Graham talked about hope for the future, that everything isn't going to end in an Armageddon (even though there will be one).

5. Wake up: Romans 13:11: "And do this, knowing the time, and now it is high time to awake out of sleep; for now our salvation is nearer than we first believed." As I look back nearly four decades after Graham shared this verse, these words seem more relevant than ever.

Responding to the Gospel

I am sure this message was well-received, as evidenced by the hundreds who streamed out of their seats when Graham gave an invitation for people to come forward and pray to receive Jesus as their Lord and Savior. Those numbers included Joe and his girlfriend. When I asked if they wanted to make that decision, they agreed, and we all walked from the stands onto the field, where they prayed with many others.

About two weeks later, Joe told me he wanted to be baptized in water in his swimming pool. I couldn't help thinking of Peter's powerful message on the Day of Pentecost when three thousand responded to the powerful move of the Holy Spirit: "Then Peter said to them, 'Repent, and let every one of you be baptized in the name of Jesus Christ for the remission of sins; and you shall receive the gift of the Holy Spirit'" (Acts 2:38).

The following Sunday, Espe and I took Chuck, my old boss from Bob Sykes Dodge, and his wife to the meeting. Graham's message touched Chuck too, and after it wrapped up, I walked with Chuck to the center of the field. When the area was totally filled, the evangelist led Chuck and the rest of the crowd in a prayer of forgiveness and repentance from their sins. Chuck took his salvation seriously, joining a church in Santa Cruz where the pastor took him under his wing. Whenever we saw him after that, Chuck demonstrated his faith through his faithful church involvement and eagerness to tell others about Jesus. Years later, Espe and I attended his funeral and spoke about his salvation day. The way in which Chuck became such a powerful witness for Christ is a memory that still shines brightly from that era.

Changes in the Wind

The year after the Graham Crusade, Joe Balestra departed from St. Claire Cadillac after Mervin Morris bought another Cadillac dealership in Fresno. Even though Joe was a minority owner in the business, Morris insisted Joe go to Fresno to run his new acquisition. Occasionally, after attending the Los Angeles auto auction sales, I would take a side trip to Fresno while heading back north to see how Joe was doing. On my first visit, he told me how sad he was over being away from

4

his family; he sounded similar notes on another stop I made a week or two later. I sensed tension behind the scenes.

In the midst of these changes, I got fired for no apparent reason. To this day, I believe the reasons didn't stem from lagging sales or anything, but my close friendship with Joe. Guilt by association, so to speak. Soon after my departure, Joe sold his stock back to Morris and bought an Oldsmobile dealership in Sunnyvale, just twelve miles from San Jose. I went to see Joe often after he returned to the area. I attended his funeral in the late 1980s at a Catholic church in Redwood City. During the service, they asked if anyone wanted to speak in memory of Joe. I went up front and told the congregation that I knew Joe was now in heaven because of his belief in Jesus Christ as his Savior.

Considering my unexpected change of fortunes at the Cadillac dealership, I was grateful that we had sold our home in Hillsborough and bought a less expensive one in Los Gatos the year before I lost my job. Although we loved our home in Hillsborough, as a family, we had prayed about moving to a place that would have enough features to be suitable for all of us. Namely, enough space for our sizable extended family, some land with trees, a treehouse for Donny, a swimming pool for Albert, and a high school close by for Charlene. Espe wanted one with five bedrooms (remember, her parents lived with us), a front iron fence, and a spacious room for our Friday prayer meetings—plus room for parking.

On her initial inspection with the real estate agent, Espe counted only three bathrooms inside the home, which could have been a problem. However, the agent then took her to the separate pool area, where Espe discovered a bathroom with a shower.

Meanwhile, I had prayed for a home with excellent carpeting and payments we could afford. At that time, mortgage rates were still at a steep 16 percent, some of the highest rates ever. Fortunately, they had backed down after topping out in 1981 at 18.5 percent amid the Federal Reserve's war with inflation. That made payments on the average home about triple what they are today. And that doesn't include the costs of property taxes, home insurance, and maintenance. As you can imagine, this put a serious damper on the housing market (another example of where the good old days weren't so good).

In what I consider another example of the Lord's favor, we were able to purchase the home by giving the owner the equity he had invested in the place and assuming his 5 percent loan, or less than one-third the prevailing interest rates. Those kinds of deals don't come along every day. Early in my Christian walk, I had learned about the benefits of tithing. Malachi 3:10-11 says:

> 'Bring all the tithes into the storehouse, that there may be food in My house, and try Me now in this,' says the LORD of hosts, 'if I will not open for you the windows of heaven and pour out for you such blessing that there will not be room enough to receive it. And I will rebuke the devourer for your sakes, so that he will not destroy the fruit of your ground, nor shall the vine fail to bear fruit for you in the field,' says the LORD of hosts.

Had it not been for God rebuking the devourer, a mortgage at triple the rate we secured could have gobbled up my paycheck.

A Saving Move

Once we got resettled in Los Gatos, we resumed hosting Friday night Bible studies. That first Friday, Espe had some help to get things set up from her cousin, Martha; her best friend, Nelleke; and a few other people. However, every time you shuffle a meeting time or location—no matter whether it involves a church, a business, or an organization—it causes an interruption in turnouts. You may remember me mentioning how we had upwards of fifty people coming to meetings in our old home. At that first meeting in Los Gatos, we had just seventeen people, many of them family or relatives.

However, we would see God's hand in this move because of the friendship we made with our next-door neighbor Mike, a former band member of a nationally known rock group. (He has since died; I am not using his last name out of respect for his family.) His wife and son would come over with him. Since his son was Donny's age, they liked to play together and often wound up in the treehouse. One night his wife showed up at our home, asking if I could come to their house to talk with Mike. He had a gun pointed at his head and declared his intentions to kill himself.

After walking over there, I warned Mike, "if you pull that trigger, you will go immediately to hell." I pleaded with him to consider life over death, talking with him for the next hour and a half. Asking the Holy Spirit for wisdom as we went back and forth, I ministered the love of God to him the best I knew. I quoted 2 Corinthians 10:3-6 to him:

> For though we walk in the flesh, we do not war according to the flesh. For the weapons of our warfare are not carnal but mighty in God for pulling down strongholds, casting down arguments and every high thing that

exalts itself against the knowledge of God, bringing every thought into captivity to the obedience of Christ, and being ready to punish all disobedience when your obedience is fulfilled.

Mike eventually calmed down and gave the gun to his wife. When we finished talking, his countenance had changed. His conversation had shifted to a more positive tone and his hope for the future. This happened on a Thursday evening; the next night, he came to our Bible study and made a public decision to follow Jesus as Savior and Lord. For a while after that, Mike came over to our house every other day. Espe would often spend two to three hours in the Bible with him because he was so hungry for knowledge and wisdom about Jesus. Espe eagerly taught him about the unconditional nature of God's love for him, which assured Mike of the Lord's complete forgiveness. Sometimes he would bring a friend to our Friday night meeting. That man asked a lot of questions, and we hope he came to know Jesus as Savior through Mike's influence.

Jim Woodall preaching.

Around the same time, we saw another break-through in our studies. A man named Rick Miller came to our first meeting and invited a gifted worship leader named Jim Woodall to make the three-hour drive from his home in Mi-Wuk Village, a picturesque little town on the edge of

the Yosemite Forest area in northeastern California. When Jim started singing, everyone attending could sense the Holy Spirit's anointing on his voice and the music. It moved our fellowship into a new, deeper dimension of worship.

After the meeting, God told Jim to help lead us in worship and prayer. So, for more than a year, he made the three-hour drive each way every week to bless us with his music.

During one of those meetings, the Lord told Jim to go into full-time ministry. Before he left for a language school in Central America, I was able to hire him at a Cadillac dealership in Menlo Park, where I worked for several months. A month before he left, Jim sold thirty-one new and used vehicles, which paid for his travel and the cost of tuition. While attending Bible school, he traveled around Nicaragua to preach the gospel, often at the risk of losing his life. There are now six churches in the region, and he still makes return trips.

In addition to Jim's stirring visit that first night, a woman from Stanford University came. She was so moved by the worship, the message from the Bible, and the unity of the group; she later brought about a dozen other Hispanic people with her. They enjoyed themselves so much that it inspired us to start a Spanish-speaking ministry in another section of our home, which met as a group after the praise and worship time.

Starting a Business

If you have ever been fired or lost your job with no adequate explanation, you know the sting of dismay and even bitterness that can follow. Especially if someone tells you, "you have one hour to pack up your desk," and then watches you like a hawk to make sure you don't take off with anything. (In my case, it wasn't quite that like, but I know people who have been dismissed with such abrupt harshness.) When the general manager of St. Claire Cadillac came to tell me I was no longer needed, he used the mysterious and lame-sounding reason: "We're going in a different direction."

When I had departed from my previous job, it had come in a fit of emotion. Now, as a believer in Christ, I vowed to avoid any rash actions or foolish decisions that could damage my witness and leave a black mark on my reputation. Seeking God's direction and wisdom, after considerable prayer, I decided to start a wholesale automotive business. It began with going to the Department of Motor Vehicles to get a license and signing up with both automotive auctions in Santa Clara County.

My daily routine consisted of getting up early and hustling out to meet used car managers to discuss their recent trade-ins and find out whether they planned to keep them to retail, place them on their used car lot, or let them go for a wholesale price. If they decided to wholesale the car, we would discuss price; if it were realistic, I would buy one, and sometimes several as a package deal. The way we priced vehicles was with the aforementioned Kelley Blue Book, which helped everyone determine a car's market value.

"A Super Sales Agent"

I had just graduated from high school in June of 1985 when I met a sister I never knew existed, kicking off a fun summer. When September drew near, I excitedly let my parents know about my plans to attend the local community college. However, it was my turn to be shocked when Pop replied: "Well, I have plans for you. You're going to wake up in the morning, and I am going to train you in how to buy cars."

Seriously? I thought he was joking! But the next day, at 4:30 a.m., he banged on my bedroom door and singing loudly: "Rise and shine and give God your glory, glory." I had to wake up if nothing more than to make him stop. There I was an hour later, driving Pop to work before my training began.

Months later, a used car manager told me how smart my father was, sending an eighteen-year-old girl out to buy cars. He was right: Pop was smart. With the industry dominated by men, no women were buying cars in our area. Granted, I faced plenty of rejection, but most of the time, I was too young and full of myself to recognize what was

**happening. Besides, I had loads of energy
to park my car, locate the used car manager,
check their trade-ins, and check the Kelley
Blue Book as I paged my father. By the time
he and I met up, I had already determined
the value of the car.**

**My dad and I were able to get more cars
and make more money with two of us going
to the dealerships and auctions in the San
Francisco Bay Area. It wasn't until later that
I realized my father was then going through
a tough time in the business, and me being
around brightened his days. Mine too.**

—Charlene Allnutt, Daughter

My own business gave me another advantage: when
our daughter, Charlene, graduated from Los Gatos High
School in 1985, I could offer her a job. Soon after that,
we were doing so well we decided to invest in a used
car lot. Taking over an existing lot at the intersection of
San Carlos Street and Bascom Avenue in San Jose, we
changed the name to B&H Automotive. Most buying of
vehicles occurred in San Jose, so I had Charlene acquire
cars from dealers ranging from Sunnyvale up to Redwood City. The vehicles that didn't go to the used car lot
went to one of the county's two auto auctions. She told
me she used to enjoy sitting next to the auctioneer and

watch me moving around the floor, chatting with various folks while our car was on the auction block.

As I just mentioned, a big advantage of working for yourself is more availability for ministry. I ended up on the board of the Christian Challenge Ministry in San Jose and (as I mentioned earlier) became the president of the FGBMI chapter. We used to have weekly luncheons in the private dining room of a popular restaurant and a monthly Friday night dinner. Those were great times of ministry to others and helped me form some fantastic friendships. Many of the businesspeople we reached out to came to know Jesus as their Savior. These experiences left me great memories of our chapter meetings, not to mention the regional and state conventions we attended in Sacramento and Southern California.

However, when I look back on our days in the greater San Jose area, I have no fonder memory than the night Mike prayed to receive Jesus as his Lord and Savior. Less than twenty-four hours earlier, he was staring down the barrel of a gun, ready to end his life and spend eternity in hell, separated forever from God. Now, I look forward to seeing him again when I return to heaven. Jesus rescued Mike's life, and we had the honor of playing a small role in his decision.

There is no more satisfying thrill than to see someone heed the words Jesus spoke to Nicodemus:

Most assuredly, I say to you, unless one is born of water and the Spirit, he cannot enter the kingdom of God. That which is born of the flesh is flesh, and that which is born of the Spirit is spirit. Do not marvel that I said to you, 'You must be born again.' The wind blows where it wishes, and you hear the sound of it, but cannot tell where it comes from and where it goes. So is everyone who is born of the Spirit.

John 3:5-8

Because Mike was born of the Spirit, he now knows the joy of dancing in heaven.

CHAPTER 8

Ministry of Love and Healing

"Grant to Your servants that with all boldness they may speak Your word, by stretching out Your hand to heal, and that signs and wonders may be done through the name of Your holy Servant Jesus." And when they had prayed, the place where they were assembled together was shaken; and they were all filled with the Holy Spirit, and they spoke the word of God with boldness.

Acts 4:29-31

With his sparkling hazel eyes, full head of hair, graceful presence, and confidence borne of an unshakable faith in God, Kenny Foreman was a larger-than-life figure. In 1965, he, along with his wife, Shirley, and their two sons left a thriving church in Kansas City, Missouri, to start a new work in California. When they took over a small church in San Jose, only thirty-two people attended their first service. The congregation soon had a new name, a new attitude, and a new vision for what God could accomplish through them.

We met in the mid-1970s because Kenny also liked to drive Cadillacs. Kenny's best friend was a used car dealer; he and I knew each other from the business, and the guy trusted me to give Kenny a good deal. So, together they made the hour-long drive to San Francisco. After I made Kenny a great offer, we shook hands, filled out the paperwork, and headed to lunch. I found myself enamored with this gregarious, smooth-talking man, who didn't even tell me what he did until we were at lunch. When I learned he pastored the Cathedral of Faith Church in San Jose, I smiled and told him I had a general rule when it came to the conversation: "Don't talk to me about Jesus."

That marked the beginning of my friendship with Kenny. He would return every two years or so to buy another Cadillac since he knew his best friend would give him top trade-in value on the one Kenny had been driving. Whenever we made a deal on a Cadillac, after completing the paperwork, Kenny and I often went to lunch. Although you might think otherwise, he honored the request I made when we first met to avoid "Jesus talk."

I think that kind of integrity and caring more about an individual's preferences than whether he made another gospel presentation is one reason Cathedral of Faith went on to become a sparkling success story. The good this church has done and the help it has given to people around the world is one of those lesser-publicized realities that deserve all kinds of attention. Although Kenny died in 2018, his son, Ken, is now senior pastor and has continued to shepherd its phenomenal growth; his brother, Kurt, is director of operations. The church has eleven campuses around the region that collectively conduct more than two hundred ministries.

Their work includes Reaching Out Ministry, which serves the homeless and needy and distributes more than sixteen million dollars in food annually. That includes providing food for families at thirty-seven public schools. Its 30,000-square-feet Family Life Center has a fitness center with cardio equipment, a weight room, and gymnasium, and organized sports and recreational activities. It also has a Prayer Center where people can pause for prayer and reflection. And a youth center with classrooms, media walls, an auditorium, and a rock-climbing wall. In 2007, it started University Preparatory Academy for students in seventh through twelfth grades. In 2019–2020, the school enrolled more than six hundred students and has made *U.S. News & World Report*'s list of "America's Best High Schools."

However, none of these kinds of accomplishments mattered that much to Kenny Foreman. At least, not in comparison to another soul entering the kingdom of heaven. The Sunday we visited Cathedral of Faith, and I shared the news that I had become a born-again Christian; he jumped for joy!

A New Home

In chapter six, I mentioned attending Crossroads Bible Church, where we started attending services regularly in March of 1980. However, after several years the Vietnamese ministry where I had been speaking dwindled because so many attendees had started working at doughnut shops on Sunday. In the meantime, we started visiting Cathedral of Faith more often, attracted by their numerous outreaches and my prior association with Kenny Foreman.

In 1984, I sensed God telling me my time at Crossroads had ended and to get involved at Cathedral of Faith. Soon after Espe and I decided to make it our church home, we got involved in the Reaching Out Ministry. Every week we would give out bags of groceries after gathering in one of the large meeting rooms. I would often deliver a fifteen-minute message explaining the way to salvation through Jesus Christ. Afterward, if anyone expressed interest in knowing more, I would refer them to a counselor for one-on-one attention. In addition to ministering one day during the week, I enrolled in the University of the Word, a series of Bible classes for lay leaders and members that Kenny launched in the mid-1980s. In June of 1987, I was part of the first class to graduate.

Espe and I also became friends there with Tony Ortiz, an ex-gang member who became an ordained minister after his release from prison. Using firsthand knowledge of gang life to minister to young people caught up in gangs, drugs, and violence, Tony founded Breakout Prison Outreach in 1981. (Now known as California Youth Outreach, today it is based in Salinas, an hour south of San Jose.) Under Tony, the ministry conducted weekly visits to several prisons and later started gang awareness weekends in state youth authority facilities.

Because of these and other activities, he became a nationally recognized expert in the field of gang intervention and prevention. In 2004, the California Wellness Foundation awarded Tony its California Peace Prize for his work with so many troubled teens and young adults. He has also been honored for his work by the city of San Jose, the California Youth Authority, and the state legislature.

While Tony was associated with Cathedral of Faith, we would invite him to speak periodically to our Friday night Bible studies in Los Gatos. He had a big heart for helping people coming out of prison to readjust to society, establishing a network of group homes so they could have a place to live and hear about Jesus. Along with housing, residents received three meals a day and clothing. As the ministry grew, Tony prayed for a van that could transport up to fifteen people; we were able to give him the vehicle as a gift.

"A Pivotal Provision"

"For I know the plans I have for you,' declares the LORD, 'plans to prosper you and not to harm you, plans to give you hope and a future."

Jeremiah 29:11 (NIV)

In the mid-1980s, my wife, Liz, and I were new to ministry when God called me to go into state-run youth facilities and inner cities to deal with kids and young adults involved in gang violence. Soon after, we received invitations to conduct special holiday events at juvenile facilities.

Naturally, coming from a gang background, I didn't have many resources. Still, a door opened to be able to take people from our church, Cathedral of Faith, to state-run detention centers. Now that I had the opportunity to go, though, I had no means of travel. How could I do it? John 10:3 says: "When we belong to God, we hear His voice." The Word also says God uses the body of Christ to get certain things done. I prayed and asked God to help me.

In response, God led me to Mark 5:1-20, about the demon-possessed man. Crying at night in torment, while people across the lake felt compassion for him, they weren't sure how to help. That is, until Jesus came their way, crossed the water, and set him free. I sensed God telling me He had the means of helping me too.

In a nutshell, that's how God led me to Buzz Howell. I went to him and explained my predicament. He put it on Buzz's heart to help our church accomplish the task of ministering to young people by giving me a vehicle to go there.

This miracle catapulted my faith to a new level and let me know God would do even greater things in my life in the future. But this marked a pivotal point in my life. I will never forget how God used this dear brother.

—*Tony Ortiz*
Breakout Prison Outreach Founder

Life Brings Surprises

When Espe's aunt Rosa and uncle Homero decided to retire in 1985 and let their sons run their motel and restaurant business in Piedras Negras, Mexico, they moved to San Jose with their daughter, Diana, and temporarily settled in a house owned by relatives. In addition to them attending our Friday night prayer meetings, we had several people from Peru, and the woman from Stanford University I mentioned in chapter seven, who would bring up a dozen Spanish-speaking people with her in a motor home.

When they first came, we had the speaker preaching a session in English and a woman named Rachel Fernandez interpreting in Spanish. However, we soon decided to worship together as a group before breaking into English- and Spanish-speaking sessions since Rachel's husband, Daniel, was a fantastic preacher who spoke Spanish. He also had the gift of prophecy, and many Hispanics in his sessions were blessed by his messages; a number of them also accepted Jesus as their Savior.

Many miracles took place during those years. One of the first involved a pastor who had a prison ministry. One night, he called out: "Someone here has a bad back because of a short leg."

That was me!

I went forward and sat on a chair in front of him as he picked up both legs and slowly tilted them in his hands, nodding as he looked. As he did, my wife rushed up to see what was happening. The pastor lifted the shorter one and prayed for it to grow. As Espe watched in amazement, it grew to normal length. (As I mentioned earlier, these kinds of healings were common during the charismatic renewal of the 1960s, '70s, and '80s.) After that happened, I had faith to pray for others with this problem and various illnesses. One night I felt God leading me to ask if any women had a "female problem." I was terrified to speak that out loud, but after gathering my courage, I asked the question. Four women came up, and all were healed.

As fantastic as those kinds of experiences were, in August of 1985, I saw God move in a way I never expected. After five years of searching and prayer, my oldest daughter, Coralee, left a message with her contact information. She had been the result of a brief romantic relationship I had with her mother prior to leaving San Jose for Azusa, where I met Espe. Coralee had just completed her first year of college at the University of New Mexico; during a visit to San Jose, her mother, an employee of the Center for Employment Training, saw my name in a magazine published by Christian Challenge Ministries, where I served on the board of directors.

I was a bit shaken when Coralee left a message. I gathered my composure and talked with my wife and children about arranging a meeting with her. Sweat was popping out from beneath my arms and collar when I sat down with my family; the initial reactions pleased me. Charlene was excited to learn she had a sister, and Albert and Donny expressed support (and surprise). Espe was a different matter, though. Although she knew I had been paying monthly child support for eighteen years, Espe never expected Coralee to want to meet us. But beyond her shock, I sensed anger brewing beneath the surface. Since Espe was due to lead a small-group Bible study that day, she left soon after without a word. But her body language broadcast her hostility.

Learning to Love

As she drove across San Jose, Espe felt ugly feelings taking hold inside her heart. Silently, she began "negotiating" with God, telling Him He had to love Coralee through me because Espe felt no love for her whatsoever. She was furious at me for even agreeing to meet with my long-lost daughter.

Just then, Espe turned on a Christian radio station and asked the Lord to speak to her through the program. Soon the pastor teaching that day spoke these words: "Though I speak with the tongues of men and of angels, but have not love, I have become sounding brass or a clanging cymbal" (1 Corinthians 13:1). The pastor's wife, who was part of his ministry, asked: "Please say it again." Espe took that as a directive from God, telling her she needed to forgive and open her heart to Coralee. When Espe did, she felt God's peace flow through her. Now she could also lead the Bible study at Terra's apartment without resentment holding her back.

A regular at our Friday night prayer and Bible study meetings, Terra had invited two friends to join her that day. As the group sat around the table, Espe had them open their Bibles to 1 John 5:14-15: "Now this is the confidence that we have in Him, that if we ask anything according to His will, He hears us. And if we know that He hears us, whatever we ask, we know that we have the petitions that we have asked of Him." Since all three of these women lived in apartments, Espe asked them if they would like a house instead of an apartment. They replied in unison with a laugh, "we barely make it now."

"Do you believe God hears us?" Espe said: "God is almighty, and He hears us."

She convinced them the Lord has the power to answer prayers, no matter how outrageous or impossible they may seem on the surface. So, each woman wrote down exactly what they wanted in a home, although only two of them believed God could make it possible. Within six months, those two had purchased a house. It wasn't just those women who experienced a breakthrough that day. As Espe walked out of that Bible study, she did so with a smile on her face, believing God would indeed help her to love Coralee.

Soon after this, we went on a previously planned vacation to Lakeport and our favorite summer activity of waterskiing on Clear Lake. I don't think anyone enjoyed themselves more that week than Espe, who felt relief from stifling anger and emotion after giving her problem to God. When we returned, I called Coralee and scheduled a luncheon meeting at the Hyatt House Hotel on First Street, just off the 101 Freeway in San Jose. When we arrived, I dropped Espe and Charlene off at the front door before going to park the car. After they went into the restaurant and met Coralee, I walked in and sat down next to Espe. As my wife introduced me to Coralee, I smiled, shook hands, and said: "I'm happy to meet you."

After these pleasantries, we joined in Charlene and Coralee's conversation about the Santa Cruz Beach Boardwalk, an amusement park about forty-five minutes southwest of San Jose. As we all chatted, though, I noticed Espe was not saying much. I later learned that was because God was answering her prayer to be able to love Coralee as God loves her. He touched Espe, and she felt rushing rivers of love flowing through her heart to Coralee. (As John 7:38 says: "He who believes in Me, as the Scripture has said, out of his heart will flow rivers of living water.") Soon Espe started telling people we had four children instead of three.

Miracles Abound

As Coralee and I talked about her first year of college in New Mexico, she expressed shock to learn that I was a gringo, since her mother had told her—because I had passed on the fib—that her father was half-Mexican. Coralee had always assumed she was more Mexican than white, but now realized she was half-white. I apologized about the past and not being there for her, but I could also see her excitement over having a sister and Espe warming up to her.

"I can live with being half-white," Coralee said with a laugh as we continued chatting over lunch. That weekend, Coralee and Charlene went to Santa Cruz, and soon after that, Coralee spent two months with us in Los Gatos. Charlene and Coralee bonded and became the sisters both had always wanted. For the last three months of 1986, Coralee also worked at my used car lot. Even better, in December of that year, she accepted Jesus Christ as her Savior at one of our Friday night prayer meetings. The woman who led Coralee to Christ was the same person Coralee talked to at Christian Challenge when she called there and left a message for me.

When Coralee graduated from the University of New Mexico in 1989 with her bachelor's degree in psychology, we were able to attend the ceremony. She would later obtain her master's degree in Latin American studies and an MBA in international management. She worked for nine years at the University of New Mexico and three years with the Nevada Department of Health. She is the mother of three girls, Sarah, Rachel, and Elizabeth (who goes by Lisa) and grandmother of three. Coralee made a career shift in 2013 and sells commercial real estate—a sales professional like her father and grandfather.

The reunion with my oldest daughter went so well; it is one more example in the series of miracles I lived through during the 1980s. I still bask in the glow of seeing friends Joe and Chuck accepting Christ at the Billy Graham Crusade and our neighbor, Mike, going from the end of a gun to deciding to follow Jesus. These incidents are living proof of the gift of the Holy Spirit and His availability to everyone who believes God still heals today as He has done countless times in the past.

While our faith wavered occasionally, we chose to go "all in" on our belief in God's power after seeing my leg grow out three-quarters of an inch. That was just one of seventeen such healings we documented in our home prayer group. After the experience, I mentioned earlier where I saw four women healed of a "female problem," my confidence in God's miracle-working power shot up 100 percent, to the same place where Espe's had always been.

To give you some examples, take the time Espe was at a women's meeting during the Christmas season when a woman came up to her and told Espe she had just gotten married after my wife prayed with her just two months earlier that the woman would find a husband. Taking Espe by the hand, the woman guided my wife across the hall to meet her husband. Espe's mouth nearly fell open as she looked at the very kind of man Espe had prayed this woman would find—brown hair, tall, handsome, and a Christian. The new bride glowed as she introduced him to Espe.

A Christian missionary was sitting in his office close by and overheard this exciting story. So, he asked if Espe could pray for a spouse for him too. She replied that he should get out a piece of paper and write down exactly what kind of wife he wanted. The man listed these qualities: 1) A petite blonde who 2) owned her own home, 3) was around fifty-five, and 4) loved riding motorcycles. After they prayed and agreed that God would put him together with such a woman, they both said, "Amen."

Five months later, a wedding invitation arrived in the mail. When Espe opened it, she saw that it was for the upcoming wedding of this missionary and his fiancé. Three weeks later, when we went to the bride's home for the wedding, the groom greeted Espe: "You will be surprised when you see my bride." When the music started and the bride walked across the backyard to the altar, Espe saw a petite blonde in her mid-fifties who owned this house. After the ceremony, the groom took Espe to the garage, where she saw two motorcycles decorated with cans and signs saying: "Newlyweds." Excited for them, Espe praised the Lord for answering this missionary's prayer.

"Meeting My Dad"

When I was in second grade, our teacher asked us to make a Father's Day card for our dads. Not having met my father, I had to imagine what he might look like. So, I drew him with a full beard.

Hindsight being 20/20, I drew my father to look like Jesus. Little did I know that twelve years later, it would in fact, be Jesus who brought my father into my life—for real.

Meeting dad for the first time was a unique, almost indescribable experience. He was so tall and stout with hazel eyes, olive skin, and a warm smile that stretched from one ear to the other. His wife, Espe, was kind but distant that day.

My other joy that day was meeting my sister, Charlene. She's eight months younger than me, and we quickly discovered that day we had many things in common. We both have beautiful olive skin, brown eyes, round faces, and freckles. We both love music, dancing, the beach, and shopping. It was like getting to meet my long-lost Irish twin!

I'm still amazed at the miracle of having my father in my life. It's because of the love of Jesus that we have the most beautiful, loving family that represents my life's treasure. And for that, I am forever grateful.

—*Coralee Quintana, Daughter*

Me surrounded by Donny, the beautiful Esperanza, Albert, Charlene, and Coralee Quintana

Powerful Prayers

Espe prayed similar prayers for her cousin Martha and several other people. Even though she is Mexican, Martha wanted a gringo who was a Christian, tall, had brown hair, and was an attorney. Espe suggested asking God that she find a man with no "baggage," meaning no ex-wife or children. Although Martha didn't have the faith for the latter request, Espe did. Martha later married a tall, white, brown-haired attorney with no ex-wife or children.

During the time I was in the hospital for my appendix operation, Espe was coming to visit me with our son, Albert. On the elevator, she ran into a mother of one of Albert's classmates from Los Gatos Christian School. That woman was on her way to say goodbye to a friend named Mary Seese, who was terminally ill with cancer. When Espe came to my room and shared her conversation about Mary's friend, I urged her to go to Mary's hospital room and pray for her.

When she reached Mary's room, Espe saw numerous machines hooked up to her body. Espe asked the husband, who was with his son and looking very sad, to write down the name of the cancer. Espe promised she would pray for Mary. As the husband jotted down the information, he said, "Well, you know that God answers prayers, and sometimes He does not."

"I don't know which God you are praying to, but my God heals everyone!" Espe said. First Peter 2:24 says that Jesus "Himself bore our sins in His own body on the tree, that we, having died to sins, might live for righteousness—by whose stripes you were healed."

Although Espe asked the man and his son to step out of the room so she could pray for Mary, he replied that he and his son wanted to stay and pray too. Espe initiated spiritual warfare against the devil, binding the enemy's power over her body and losing God's power. Meanwhile, Mary's husband called out three Scriptures from the Bible as he agreed with Espe's prayer. Afterward, Espe returned to my room to tell me what had happened.

That year at Christmas time, we went to Los Gatos Christian Church for the children's Christmas concert. A woman came up to us before it started and asked Espe if she recognized her.

"No, I don't," Espe said. "I'm so sorry."

"I'm Mary Seese.

Espe almost fainted. Mary looked beautiful and full of life. Her faith had been restored, and Mary promised to pray for others when she totally recovered. As I relate this true story, just think for a minute: What are the odds that Mary would be in the same hospital at the same time I had my appendicitis attack, and my wife ride the same elevator at the same time as Mary's friend, and then go to Mary's room to pray, and see Mary healed? I doubt the oddsmakers in Las Vegas would even take that bet. No matter what the odds, a prayer of faith ended with a fantastic result!

The Rewards of Obedience

As I reflect on these days, I believe one reason we saw the Spirit move in such powerful ways is our obedience to follow His leading in our lives. We knew that God is an all-powerful, all-knowing, miracle-working Lord. Our primary role was to submit to His Lordship so He could work through us.

I took a primary step of obedience early in my Christian life by submitting to His direction to get immersed in water, in a rite known as baptism. This is a key step for every born-again Christian since it is based on what Jesus did before launching His public ministry:

> Then Jesus came from Galilee to John at the Jordan to be baptized by him. And John tried to prevent Him, saying, 'I need to be baptized by You, and are You coming to me?' But Jesus answered and said to him, 'Permit it to be so now, for thus it is fitting for us to fulfill all righteousness.' Then he allowed Him. When He had been baptized, Jesus came up immediately from the water; and behold, the heavens were opened to Him, and He saw the Spirit of God descending like a dove and alighting upon Him. And suddenly a voice came from

heaven, saying, 'This is My beloved Son, in whom I am well pleased'

Matthew 3:13-17

When I came to the Lord and learned about baptism, I knew that had to be my next step. When I shared my decision with Espe and our children, she, Charlene, Albert, and Donny all expressed their desire to be baptized too. We picked a Sunday when Crossroads Bible Church had a full house after verifying that our friend Bob Rausch could perform the ceremony. The crowd clapped their hands each time one of us came out of the water. Each of us sensed in our hearts that we did the right thing, in God's way and with His approval.

Taking advantage of our indoor swimming pool in Los Gatos, we baptized many people during our Friday night meetings, announcing special baptism nights in advance. One of the first persons I baptized was my neighbor, Mike, the former rock band musician who had threatened to kill himself. Jim Woodall and I baptized Rick and Leslie, two faithful supporters of our small ministry. Throughout the years, we saw many people receive Jesus as their Savior at our meetings, and we performed water baptisms.

Water baptisms

Such experiences are why I can say as King David did:

> Bless the LORD, O my soul; and all that is within me, bless His holy name! Bless the LORD, O my soul, and forget not all His benefits: who forgives all your iniquities, who heals all your diseases, who redeems your life from destruction, who crowns you with loving kindness and tender mercies, who satisfies your mouth with good things, so that your youth is renewed like the eagle's.
>
> Psalm 103:1-5

While my body may be getting old, I still know the joy of feeling renewed like an eagle!

CHAPTER 9

A Life of Joy

For we are members of His body, of His flesh and of
His bones. 'For this reason a man shall leave his fa-
ther and mother and be joined to his wife, and the
two shall become one flesh.' This is a great mystery,
but I speak concerning Christ and the church. Nev-
ertheless let each one of you in particular so love his
own wife as himself, and let the wife see that she
respects her husband.

Ephesians 5:30-33

When Charlene came to Espe and me with the news
that she and Frank Allnutt had gone to Reno, Nevada, on
the Fourth of July of 1987 and gotten married, I couldn't
help having flashbacks to 1966. Few people expected our
marriage to last following the impulsive decision Espe
and I made to run off to Las Vegas. But after watching
the happiness we enjoyed through the years, Charlene
figured she and Frank could make it too.

A native of England, Frank was born in Crawley, a city about thirty miles south of London. He and his friend Glyn had flown to New York to tour the city before going to Mexico for a month to visit a friend of Glyn in Monterrey. Next, they headed north to Sunnyvale (twelve miles west of San Jose) to visit Glyn's brother, Phil. Since they were broke, they secured jobs at the car wash in town. That's where Charlene used to go for a car wash, and it was literally love at first sight.

While they wanted to get married sooner than they did, Frank had to return to England for a few months. He had been in the US illegally and went back home to obtain a visa. They eloped to Reno after he returned because Charlene didn't want to live together before they were married. She spilled the news to us a month later when our family went to Lakeport to enjoy a weekend of waterskiing. Fortunately, we had always liked Frank. He had met us nine months earlier as we were leaving our home in Los Gatos to take part in a Christmas play staged by Cathedral of Faith. I was dressed up as one of the three kings and Espe as a maiden. To say he was blown away would be an understatement! He talked about it for years afterward.

Espe's reaction to Charlene's Nevada venture was nearly identical to her mother's when she had learned of Espe's Las Vegas wedding: "Now you two have to get married in a church."

Frank and Charlene agreed to continuing their plans to having a wedding in Cathedral of Faith. Soon after, Frank and Charlene went to Cathedral of Faith to talk with Ken Foreman (Kenny Foreman Jr.), who agreed to perform the ceremony on October 10. I asked Frank and Charlene, "would you rather have twenty-five thousand dollars for a down payment on a home?" Giving me a "what are you thinking?" kind of look, Charlene replied, "you only get married in a church once."

"Love of My Life"

I met the love of my life during my days on dad's car lot. Frank and I met in November of 1986 and started dating immediately, but then quickly broke up. When I told dad, he got upset, telling me, "You blew it, Char!"

Around Valentine's Day, Frank and I started dating again. We saw each other every day until mid-April when the immigration service tracked him down and gave him forty-eight hours to leave. He hadn't entered the US legally.

Since my mother is from Mexico, I was very familiar with the ordeal of deportation. I went to the bank and took out the money for Frank to buy a one-way ticket to England.

We spent the day together in San Francisco before I dropped him off at the airport.

While driving to the car lot, my heart began to ache. The tears flowed. When I got to the lot, dad called mom, his voice trembling—he didn't know what was wrong. My mother had to reveal the truth: I was madly in love. Yet here I was, twenty years old, and I had no idea how to place a call to England. Instead, Frank called me and let me know he was going to come back. He kept his word. Six weeks later, he returned and quickly asked me to marry him.

It didn't take long for us to decide to elope on the Fourth of July, even though we had started planning a wedding. My family loved teasing me about marrying an English man on the day America declared independence from the redcoats.

We had our big wedding on October 10, 1987. We have some great memories,

photographs, and an old video of that day. But I still regret not taking dad's offer to skip the wedding and use the money for a down payment on a house.

Once again, he had given me some good advice.

—*Charlene Allnutt, Daughter*

With that in mind, Charlene, Espe, and I agreed: "Let's go all out." We decided on the newly opened Le Baron Hotel on North First Street since it had a great restaurant and reception area.

Wedding Bells

First came the wedding at Cathedral of Faith. Memories of that day are still among my favorites of all time. The groomsmen wore black tuxedos and Frank a white one, with the bridesmaids dressed in black-and-white gowns. Frank's best man was Glyn, his best friend who flew in from England along with Frank's brother, Charles. As everyone stood up and I looked at Charlene—and how beautiful she looked in her fashionable white wedding dress—tears came to my eyes.

"I love you," I said in a soft voice choked with emotion. "I'm so happy to be your father."

Naturally, aside from Espe, I felt that Charlene was the most beautiful bride I had ever seen. As we walked slowly down the aisle, the smiling faces of approval from everyone made us feel so grateful and blessed. Everything seemed perfect until we reached the altar and started up the stairs. Suddenly Charlene tripped, but to the relief of everyone at the wedding party, she quickly regained her balance. Thanks to his down-home manner and broad smile, Pastor Ken did a fantastic job of making all the guests relax and feel at home.

Espe and her parents, along with my mother and me, cried often. But we laughed through our tears since we were filled with joy for Charlene and Frank, who thoroughly enjoyed the ceremony. When Ken finished leading them through their vows and pronounced them husband and wife, thunderous applause and expressions of joy echoed through the church as the bride and groom walked down the aisle. Outside, everyone laughed, threw rice, and shouted their best wishes.

Before the reception at the hotel, the couple, their attendants, and family members stopped at San Jose's Municipal Rose Garden, located at Naglee and Dana avenues. Later named "America's Best Rose Garden" in an All-America Rose Selections competition, this gorgeous 5.5-acre tract is dedicated specifically to roses, with 189 varieties and more than 3,500 plantings. It was the perfect setting for the photographer to take a series of romantic photos of Frank and Charlene, family, and close friends. As I looked around the park, the beautiful roses and scenery combined with the splendor of the day nearly took my breath away.

Then came the reception at the Le Baron Hotel. Ironically, it was located just three blocks from 4th Street Bowl, my teenage bowling alley and pool hall hangout. The hotel's second floor had a banquet room with plenty of space for a large group and a spacious dance floor that quickly got put into use. Just as we arrived in the lobby, so did the mariachi band. Moments later, we reached the second floor, eyes widening when we saw the breathtaking, six-tiered wedding cake. Before long, the mariachi band started playing, with some people dancing while others sat and chatted with family and friends. At seven o'clock, waiters started serving meals of prime rib, fish, and chicken.

After dinner, Charlene's cousin Louis Lopez spun records and served as the disc jockey, with many guests again taking to the dance floor. In the midst of the reverie, Charlene cut a slice of cake while Frank surprised her after cutting his and smashing the slice into her face. Laughing, she got him back by jamming cake into his face. As the restaurant staff passed out slices to the guests, Charlene's sister, Coralee, went with her to the bathroom to clean up Charlene's face from the cake episode. The evening included the ritual of the bride throwing her bouquet toward the single women. The daughter of Rick and Leslie, two regular attendees at our Friday night Bible studies, caught it. Then came the garter throw; when Frank threw it up in the air, Espe's cousin's boyfriend caught it.

We finally called an end to the festivities at midnight.

Peaceful Atmosphere

I found other joy in my personal and business life. As I mentioned in chapter seven, because of success with my car wholesaling business, in 1986 I had opened a used car lot at San Carlos Street and Bascom Avenue. Because of the decision to follow Christ that I had made in 1979, I loved being able to operate a business that reflected Christian principles. Because I stayed so busy with auto auctions and acquiring vehicles from various dealers, I hired a Christian brother to manage the business, another one as a salesman, and even a Christian mechanic. Espe's sister Emma also worked there. Naturally, the staff had the freedom to talk to customers about Jesus; besides buying vehicles from us, many accepted Jesus as their Savior.

Many times—either before or after someone bought a car or truck—a staff member would call on me to share about my conversion experience and ensuing Christian walk. Along with the no high-pressure environment, this helped create such a positive atmosphere most customers felt relaxed and fairly comfortable. Many remarked about how different our lot was compared to others where they had gone to look at cars.

My wife loved being there to visit Emma and talk with other staff members, and many customers liked the idea of the owner's wife being involved in the business. After my visits to the used car managers at various dealerships or auto auctions, I usually made it to the lot by late afternoon. Espe and I would meet and discuss when to pick up checks from dealers who had bought the more expensive cars; sometimes, we drove to auction offices to pay for cars we had purchased or take pink slips to them to collect our checks. Meanwhile, our Friday night ministry was still going strong, even though Jim Woodall (who I mentioned in chapter seven) finally stopped leading music because of his decision to go into full-time ministry.

During my wholesale career—prior to opening my own car lot—owners of different dealerships would call, asking for my help in turning their business around and increasing sales to enhance their profitability. But before I started this kind of consulting work, I spent ninety days at Roger Penske Cadillac in Menlo Park. That's where I hired Jim as a sales representative, who took to sales like a duck to water. Selling thirty-one new or used Cadillacs his last month there helped fund his language school studies in Costa Rica. Jim said God did that for him.

After Penske Cadillac, I also helped Carl Chevrolet on Capitol Expressway, a hotbed of automotive sales activity in San Jose. I spent ninety days in their used car department, helping them refine their sales techniques and procedures and boosting their sales.

Another time, my old boss, Don Lucas, called. We made a ninety-day agreement where I helped him with his Mitsubishi dealership on Stevens Creek, about a block from his Honda dealership. Ironically, when I walked into the Mitsubishi dealership, about eight people quit and walked out. I asked the manager who stayed what happened; he told me they were doing things they knew I wouldn't approve of and wanted to go somewhere where they would feel more comfortable.

In addition to hiring new salespeople, I spent hours on basic training techniques with those who stayed. The first thing I taught them was to always introduce yourself, ask the customer's name, and build rapport with a compliment, whether that was about something they were wearing, about a child with them, or something about their family. I told them to spend two to five minutes getting to know a little bit about the customer. I spent most of my training time on these seven steps:

1. Be natural and care about what the customer needs or wants. If your customer likes you, it is because you care about them, making the next steps easier and natural.

2. Discover what type of vehicle they are looking for, including the model.

3. While going to inventory to find their make and model, keep building rapport.

4. When you find the right vehicle, pull it out to the aisle and "circle sell," starting with the styling and moving to features, benefits, safety, and equipment.

5. Demonstrate via a test drive.

6. Guide customers to the showroom floor.

7. Take customers to your office to write up the sale.

With the sales staff and manager completely trained, the dealership started selling cars in record numbers, both new and used. After our ninety-day agreement ended, Don wanted to change my plan, so we parted ways while remaining friends.

Ministry of Life

When Jim Woodall left our Friday night home meetings to go into full-time ministry, a man named Clay took over, with Greg playing guitars as they led praise and worship.

Two young women named Leslie and Joanie backed up Clay with vocals. Everyone loved singing, especially the old familiar tune "When the Saints go Marching In," when we would all get up and march around the room. God always showed up through praise and worship because He has a tremendous love for those who worship Him with all their heart and soul.

We had several people stay with us during those days in Los Gatos. At the time we started hosting meetings, we were also involved with the Vietnamese ministry at Crossroads Bible Church in San Jose. Our Friday night meetings and Sunday morning ministry often crossed paths.

One Sunday at Crossroads, we talked at the end of the Vietnamese service with a couple named Haut and Hung, who had suffered serious abuse at the hands of family members. After hitting them so violently their arms turned black and blue, a relative threw them out of the house. We were so upset at the people who did this that after praying with this couple, we offered this couple and their two young children temporary lodging in our home.

Another man who helped with the Vietnamese ministry and overheard everything we had been talking about volunteered to help Haut and Hung bring their belongings to Los Gatos. Our new guests were quite helpful around our home, cleaning, and cooking, and even helping make tamales at Christmastime. They stayed with us for eight months. During that time, they shared many stories with Espe about the cruelty of the Communists in Vietnam. Once, North Vietnamese soldiers came into their village and gathered up all the grandmothers, put them in the middle of the village, and fired their rifles until all the elderly women were dead. After this happened, Haut and Hung left for California.

Twenty years after they left our home and moved to the Los Angeles area, we went to visit them. The memory of seeing what God had done in their lives during the interim still takes my breath away. To start with, they related their story in perfect English instead of the broken dialect they had used in Los Gatos. Although initially staying with relatives, they soon moved out. Through careful saving and prudent planning, they were able to open a jewelry business in Glendale, about eight miles north of downtown Los Angeles. In addition to a prosperous business, Haut and Hung owned their own home in Arcadia, a car, and a business van. God truly blesses His people.

After this couple had left our home, close friends of ours named John and Nelleke stayed with us for three weeks while they were in between moving from one house to another. After they left, their son, John-John, came to stay with us for three more weeks.

During his time with us, John-John prevented a break-in at our home by the former boyfriend of a woman named Sandra. She had moved in with us to escape their abusive relationship. One morning as Sandra was taking her daughter to school, she saw her ex-boyfriend at the bottom of the hill. Turning around, she sped back up the street to our house, opened the door with her key, locked it, and ran upstairs to Charlene's room. There she hid in the closet with her daughter. Meanwhile, her ex stayed right behind her in hot pursuit. When he reached our house and found the door locked, he broke the kitchen window. Espe immediately called the police. While they responded within a few minutes, they said they could not arrest the intruder because they didn't see the crime. Since John-John did, though, the cops said he could make a citizen's arrest. Once John-John did, the police handcuffed him and took him away.

Gift of Prayer

We never knew how much God would bless us when we offered our home as a temporary shelter to those in need. This life of joy felt like riding a spiritual wave that could take us further than the surf in the Pacific Ocean. One of the many miracles we experienced happened after Espe prayed during a Friday night meeting. A woman named Karla had a friend who wanted her boyfriend to move out of her home. The reason: he was growing so much marijuana, the plants had overtaken every room in the apartment. As she prayed, God brought to Espe's mind the idea to visualize the plants as dead. She spoke this during prayer, and after they had prayed for a while, Karla said that she could indeed see the weeds lying on their side, lifeless.

The next morning, Karla called Espe with exciting news: her friend's boyfriend had moved out because his marijuana plants had died!

"It's all your fault," he said with a snarl as he left.

Karla said her friend wanted to meet my wife. The following Friday night, after Karla introduced her to

Espe, the friend said, "you're the one!" Then she reached out to give Espe a huge hug.

Another time, Espe received a prayer request from a close friend named Elizabeth. Elizabeth believed that if my wife prayed for her, something would happen. Tired of being barely able to survive and forced to pinch pennies to make it to the end of every month, Elizabeth told Espe she wanted ten thousand dollars "with no strings attached." So in a prayer of agreement, Espe and Elizabeth prayed for this to happen, using Matthew 16:19 as the basis: "And I will give you the keys of the kingdom of heaven, and whatever you bind on earth will be bound in heaven, and whatever you loose on earth will be loosed in heaven."

Later, Elizabeth called and asked if she could come over to our house to share some exciting news. Soon after she and Espe had prayed, the attorney for Elizabeth's aunt in New York City called Elizabeth to tell her that her aunt wanted to send her a check for ten thousand dollars! The evening she came to our house, Elizabeth hadn't opened the envelope from the attorney; she wanted Espe to see it and rejoice with her. As Elizabeth held the envelope in the air, Espe told her to open it. With hands shaking, Elizabeth slowly tore open the seal. Inside was a letter from the attorney and the check for ten thousand dollars. In a split second,

Espe and Elizabeth were jumping up and down as they celebrated.

"Hallelujah to God!" said Espe, who praised God for this answer to prayer and His faithfulness to her friend. They had just seen the living fulfillment of Matthew 18:19: "Again I say to you that if two of you agree on earth concerning anything that they ask, it will be done for them by My Father in heaven."

Spiritual Cleansing

Not only did we see miraculous provision develop more than once in response to prayer, but Espe also had a gift of faith to spiritually cleanse a person's home. A family friend in San Jose had suffered the tragic death of a sister in their family. The nurse that had been caring for the deceased woman and the family's bedridden mother said that she heard footsteps going upstairs to the deceased sister's bedroom for the last two nights. Naturally, the sounds had frightened her—badly.

Espe told the woman that there were evil spirits in that house. She told this family that she had spiritually cleaned other people's homes in the name of Jesus. She mentioned The Name in Combat, a 1979 book written by the founder of the Rhema Bible Training Center, Kenneth E. Hagin. It teaches that the name of Jesus is to be used against unseen, devilish forces that surround us.

Espe told them that we have authority in the name of
Jesus against all powers of darkness. As Mark 16:17 says:

> And these signs will follow those who believe:
> In My name they will cast out demons; they
> will speak with new tongues; they will take up
> serpents; and if they drink anything deadly,
> it will by no means hurt them; they will lay
> hands on the sick, and they will recover.

Espe explained that every child of God is part of
"those who believe," and since these signs are done
"in My (Jesus) name," they must belong to every child
of God. The two sisters asked Espe if she would go to
their mother's home to spiritually cleanse it. She told
the sisters to go to the grocery store on the way to their
mother's house and pick up some olive oil and three
empty boxes.

When they all arrived and walked into the home,
Espe told the women to take anything inside that was
evil or satanic and place it in the boxes they had picked
up at the grocery store. Searching around the house,
Espe found a satanic bible, which at first she mistook
for a regular Bible. When she opened the cover of the
satanic scriptures, Espe sensed a dark and cold spirit
coming out of it and threw it in the box as quickly as
possible. As the others looked around, the women found

a satanic prayer chair, an Ouija board, two paintings of black cats, and many evil books and figures. They tossed everything into the boxes until they were filled.

Then Espe took the olive oil and put it on her fingers as she went around every room downstairs. Anointing various places with oil, she called on the name of Jesus to rest on everything she touched and to fill every room. Then they went upstairs. When they reached the last room upstairs, which was the deceased sister's room, the telephone—which was not connected—rang. Everyone screamed and hugged Espe until it stopped ringing. Espe anointed everything in the deceased sister's room with oil, from the closets, doors, windows, and drawers to every stick of furniture.

Then everyone went downstairs to carry the boxes out. Right after they came back inside, the doorbell rang. Two women had come to pick up the satanic bible and satanic prayer chair. When they left, the nurse accepted Jesus Christ as her Savior. The women's mother, who had been in a coma for four years, awakened and whispered to her daughter, "Water." Espe prayed for her health and then led her in a prayer to accept Jesus as her Savior.

Fantastic, right? Well, yes, but life has a way of dishing out adversity and setbacks along with such triumphs.

"Casting Out Demons"

"Then He called His twelve disciples together and gave them power and authority over all demons, and to cure diseases."
Luke 9:1

The spiritual cleansing Buzz writes about here is only one of a series I have participated in; I do this because of my love for people in bondage to our spiritual enemy. I have always trusted in the name of Jesus to purify and cleanse evil, with Luke 9:1 as my gospel for healing and cleansing of body, soul, or homes.

This verse immediately came to mind when a woman approached me at one of our Friday night meetings in Los Gatos. She asked if I could pray for her granddaughter, who lived with her mother in nearby Santa Clara. The granddaughter had gone out with a man who was a satanic priest, but she didn't learn this until they had dated for a few weeks. When she tried to break it off, he refused to be rejected.

Finally, she added more locks to the doors and windows. Yet, from time to time, he reappeared. She would scream and threaten to call the police, but he always vanished before she could grab the phone. After talking with her concerned grandmother, I obtained permission to enter the home to cleanse it.

Three days later, a spiritual partner accompanied me there. Once there, we surveyed rooms before I pulled out some olive oil and started to pray. Placing oil in the shape of a cross on all the doorframes and windows that I passed by, I said repeatedly, "Faith in the name of Jesus!"

I told the woman's granddaughter that any satanic items needed to be removed right away. After this cleansing ritual, that satanic priest never showed up at her home again.

—Espe Howell, Wife

CHAPTER 10

Gone with the Wind

To everything there is a season, a time for every
purpose under heaven: a time to be born, and a
time to die; a time to plant, and a time to pluck
what is planted; a time to kill, and a time to heal; a
time to break down, and a time to build up; a time
to weep, and a time to laugh; a time to mourn, and
a time to dance; a time to cast away stones, and a
time to gather stones; a time to embrace, and a time
to refrain from embracing; a time to gain, and a
time to lose.

Ecclesiastes 3:1-6

One of the toughest lessons I learned as a follower of
Christ is that not everyone who claims to be a "brother"
is indeed faithful to God. In our case, Espe and I were
deceived twice by brothers within the same period of
time, which led to serious financial losses. In addition

to having to let go of my business at a fire-sale price, we also had to downsize and put our Los Gatos home up for sale. As tough as that pill was to swallow, I had to accept the truth of Ecclesiastes 3:1-6. Namely, that there is a time and a season for everything. Sometimes you have to let go of things, no matter how they came your way or how much you enjoyed them while you had them. In our case, the old saying, "sadder but wiser," would prove quite true.

The first setback came when I allowed a smooth-talking employee to persuade me to start carrying the loans for B&H Automotive's sales in-house instead of using a loan company to handle customers' purchases. Some of the people we sold cars to had less-than-stellar credit, but the loan company would take the loan, regardless of a customer's credit rating. The tradeoff came when the loan company also took a thousand dollars off the top to handle the financing of each car, leaving us with lower margins. At first, underwriting our own loans sounded more profitable. But it didn't take long for what turned out to be a house of cards to collapse.

At that time, a typical down payment on a used car would run between three hundred and five hundred dollars. While supposedly taking down payments and arranging financing, the guy who talked me into using this arrangement soon started pocketing monthly payments. Apparently, he persuaded people to give him the money while telling them he would "take care of it." I think he grabbed several customers' down payments along the way too, although ultimately, the paper trail got so convoluted I can't say for sure.

It only took about eight months for his fraudulent activities to surface. A year-end audit uncovered the truth of what was happening, although I had already suspected something was amiss when I started running short of capital to buy cars at auto auctions or make transactions with other dealers.

The average person who hasn't operated a business may not understand how such a thing could happen, but it isn't that difficult, especially when crooked con artists know how to cover their tracks, if only temporarily. I read news stories regularly about unethical bookkeepers or accountants who write company checks to phony suppliers or themselves and others who run up personal charges on a company credit card. Some go as far as taking a vacation on the company's account. I've never understood how such swindlers expect to get it away with it since many of them get caught. That's eventually what happened with this guy. After I fired him, he worked the same swindle at two more car lots until the second dealer prosecuted him, and he wound up going to prison. In the end, I had to sell B&H to another car dealer that offered to take over our lease for twenty-five thousand dollars.

A Hot Tamale

If that pill was hard to swallow, imagine when it happened to Espe around the same time, my employee was stealing from me. Not only did she work in a great Mexican restaurant when we met, but Espe also proved her cooking talent after we tied the knot. One of her specialties was making tamales, thanks to a great recipe handed down from her grandmother to her mother and then to her. She loved making them so much that, periodically, she and I had discussed the possibility of Espe opening her own restaurant so she could serve her tamales.

Then came what appeared to be a serious offer from my old boss Chuck. He was one of the folks I had taken to the Billy Graham crusade and, on that day, said a conversion prayer. One day Chuck dropped by the house when Espe and a couple of friends were making tamales. His eyes growing wide as he bit into the tasty delights, Chuck asked Espe if she could make five hundred of them for a big auto auction that was coming up the following week. She came through. Afterward, Chuck told her they had gone like hotcakes; he said he could have sold twice as many. Without knowing what he was getting into, Chuck declared his intention to start a restaurant with Espe near downtown Los Gatos.

Through his attorney, Chuck found a location on the main boulevard, just a few blocks from our home. He promised to handle all the expenses of launching the business and make Espe a partner in return for her serving as his chef. After leasing the building from his attorney, Chuck took Espe all over town to help him buy all the fixtures, furnishings, and equipment needed to open the doors. Within a few months, they had hired a four-member staff, with Espe conducting the interviews and finding the right people.

The day of the grand opening, the take-out-only restaurant opened at 8:00 a.m. and saw a steady stream of customers until nine o'clock that evening. That day nearly three hundred people came through the doors, with all the employees leaving happy but exhausted from the long hours. Espe was worn out too but didn't complain, even after the long hours continued day after day and week after week. After all, she was pursuing her passion and loving it, especially all the compliments that came her way from grateful customers.

Unlike the car lot, it didn't take nearly as long for things to unravel. Two months after it opened, Chuck claimed he couldn't make any money from the restaurant and sold it to a real estate saleswoman for fifty thousand dollars. However, he never paid Espe a dime for her efforts. The real estate woman had no idea of what she was getting into, either. Within six months, she closed the doors.

"Cheated again," Espe said with a sad look on her face when she came home the day everything fell apart. "After I helped him buy all the equipment and interviewed everyone to pick the right employees, and worked two months for free, all because of his promise. And he told the woman who bought it that I came with the restaurant. Well, guess what? I didn't!"

After quitting, Espe took Chuck to small claims court, which at that time had a limit of five thousand dollars; otherwise, lawsuits had to go to a higher court. Unlike typical court cases that could drag on for years, this one took only sixty days to come before a judge. Despite a valid claim, Espe wound up losing because she had never signed a contract and didn't have anything else in writing to back up her assertions.

Long after the case was dismissed, Chuck admitted he had lied about their arrangement on the stand. He confessed that when he did, he could sense Espe praying. Sweating, nervous, and shaky on the stand, he felt like spiritual arrows were raining down from heaven, punishing him for lying about one of God's servants. After the court case, a close friend of Chuck's told him, "you really owe her something." Finally, he gave Espe a three-year-old Cadillac Seville.

Losing Our Home

The loss of capital and income from both calamities forced us to put our Los Gatos home on the market. Ironically, the real estate woman we selected to handle the sale was the same one who had lost the Mexican restaurant after buying it from Chuck. (On the positive side, it took only a few weeks for our home to sell. The buyers turned it into a crisis pregnancy center for teenage girls who wanted to give birth to their babies instead of having an abortion.)

Two weeks before we had to move, we got on the phone to dozens of people to let them know the next Friday night's meeting would be our last one. We had a packed house, with even some people from Burlingame and Hillsborough coming to praise God with us. A friend named Roger, who usually supplied the doughnuts for these meetings, had to make extra ones that night. The praise and worship went for an hour. After it concluded, many people came up to share their stories about coming to know Jesus during our meetings. Despite the sadness of having to leave our home, it was a great night of rejoicing over all the great things God had done through His ministry.

"Miracles, Healings, and Salvation"

Even though this Friday night in Los Gatos marked our final time together, the joy
of the Lord filled our home. At least one hundred people—plus children—showed up. We
fellowshipped for a half-hour before breaking into song once musicians Leslie, Joni,
and Greg took their places. They led us in
such songs as "Amazing Grace," "Awesome
God," and "Blessed Assurance."

We sang and worshiped the Lord in one
accord that night, demonstrating the truth of
1 Corinthians 12:7-11. The passage talks about
the manifestations of the Spirit being given
to His people through such gifts as words of
wisdom, words of knowledge, healings, and
miracles. We had seen all these and more in
operation during our five years together.

After worship, many people came up to
testify to accepting Jesus as Savior at our
home meetings. Some experienced the
cleansing of sin through baptism in our indoor pool. Others described marriages being
saved through Christian counsel of some in
our group, as well as my husband and me.
Others told of how I ministered to their faith,

persuading them God could conqueror any sin. Our ministry to women saved countless marriages and families.

One of my favorite miracles involved a woman who had asked me to pray for her husband, who had been imprisoned for a long time. Her request: his early release. As we finished praying, he showed up at our front door. Sometimes God answers prayer quickly! We both stood there in shock and disbelief. While she hugged her husband in an iron grip, I watched, unable to speak. Whoever thinks God can't work miracles should have been there that night!

—*Esperanza (Espe) Howell, Wife*

For a while after that, we rented a condo at a new tennis club in Los Gatos before buying a home—much smaller this time—off Almaden Expressway in San Jose. One reason we chose it was its proximity to Cathedral of Faith Church.

Soon after everything had collapsed, I received a call from Tim, an industry acquaintance who owned a Chevrolet dealership on Capitol Expressway in San Jose. During a ninety-day term of employment, I helped him resolve a major problem on his used car lot by selling some of his inventory to other dealers or moving them out to auto auctions. I also fired up the sales staff, inspiring them to increase their sales to retail customers.

At the end of my time at the Chevrolet store, I received another call from my old boss Don Lucas. He was having some problems at his Cadillac dealership, which had moved about five miles away from its old location to a new building along "auto row" in Colma, just south of San Francisco. At his new lot, Don had added Acura models, but vehicle sales overall had fallen below expectations. I made a deal with his company for a base salary plus a bonus based on sales performance.

Once I started working at the dealership, I saw the first thing they needed to add was training for the sales staff, along with more salespeople. The general manager called the advertising manager of the group. At a lunch meeting close to the dealership, the advertising manager told the general manager they would need at least seventy-five thousand dollars a month for advertising to accomplish his goal.

Thanks to being able to train and hire the right staff, our sales of Acuras saw a healthy increase. I worked the desk and trained another young man to help me; he proved as talented as Larry Newman, my old friend from our 4th Street Bowl days. This young man was capable and competent when it came to putting together a deal. Nor was he afraid to go out and try additional persuasion with a customer if a salesperson wasn't able to close a sale. While everything proceeded well for about five months, Don finally got upset about the advertising expenses we used to stimulate sales, telling me he would have to cut out my salary from the group.

"No problem," I told him and walked out. After all, we had been through; I knew God would open another door for me.

Landing on My Feet

Soon after, Larry Newman called me. He was now the general manager at a new Toyota dealership in San Jose. Knowing I was looking for a job or a dealership where I could get involved in management, Larry told me to call Steve Bergstrom. Based in Santa Cruz, Steve owned a Honda and Acura dealership. Steve had tried to buy the Toyota dealership where Larry worked but lost out because of a higher bid from Larry's boss.

I called Steve and gave him a rundown of my background.

"I'm still looking for another store," he said. "Why don't you come over here?"

After we talked in person, I agreed with his suggestion that I manage Steve's Acura store. I took along my son-in-law, Frank, to see how he would like the business. Not only did he love it, but Frank also became a great salesman. He could close a sale with a flair and excelled at everything he did, eventually becoming a sales manager.

During the three months that I managed Steve's Acura dealership, he and I went to look at a Honda store in Salinas. Although Steve hoped to purchase it, we learned that day that the owner had already started negotiations to sell it to Sam Linder, who owned a Ford store in Vancouver, Washington. Soon after we visited Salinas, I received a call from Sam, who had heard about me through my visit to the Honda store. He liked what he learned about my experience in the car business and offered me an opportunity to become the general manager of that Honda dealership.

The move to Salinas proved to be one of the best I ever made. Not only did we achieve profitability in several months, but a few weeks after starting, Sam Linder sent me to Florida for five days of management training. It taught me things I never forgot, and that helped me in future endeavors. You may remember, in the previous chapter, I outlined some sales tools I taught at a Mitsubishi dealership during one of my short-term agreements. Yet hearing them emphasized, along with instruction on some new ones, helped expand my knowledge and awareness of good techniques.

The ten primary points the two trainers reviewed the first day:

1. You need to count your customers. How are you going to know how you are doing if you don't keep a count of visitors, so you know how many guests came into your dealership?
2. What are their names, and how did they hear about your place of business?
3. Salespersons should always introduce themselves and build rapport with customers through a compliment; try to make a friend.
4. Slowly walk to the area where the vehicle is located as you keep building rapport.
5. Do everything possible to find the right vehicle that fits their needs, desires, and pocketbook.
6. Walk around the vehicle to display it and explain all its features and benefits.
7. Once they find the proper vehicle, the salesperson should test-drive it first to make sure everything is running properly, and you can point out some of the interior features.
8. Pullover at a safe area at some point to let one of them drive.
9. If they desire the vehicle you drove, first, take down all of the information, mileage, stock number, price, and—if used—the license plate number. If the customer wants to keep looking, treat that as positive and continue helping them to find the right unit that will fit their needs.

10. Once you have the desired vehicle, go to your office to write up the necessary paperwork for an offer to buy at the desired price and payment.

While these things may sound basic, the trainers spent the whole day detailing each point and repeatedly going over them until they became a believer. I absorbed every detail and asked numerous questions during class and afterward while on breaks.

A Key Step

I already believed in using female up-counters—greeters who keep a close count of customers coming onto the lot and chatting with them before directing them to a sales rep. I had been successful in the past as a general manager using women to interact with customers and get initial information. They would ask such questions as "What brought you into the dealership?" "Do you live in the area?" "How long have you been here?" "Where do you work?" "What size of family do you have?" They were really hospitable and detail-oriented.

Not only did they tally the number of customers coming through the doors, but these up-counters also helped me track what happened during the process by recording such information as whether the salesperson took a demo drive, explained all the car's features and benefits, how long they spent with customers, and if they covered all the steps in the process.

The trainers also helped me better understand the steps in hiring up-counters and what they need to do to be successful. Things like whether they smile (a lot of people don't), have a good personality and attitude, dress properly, are diplomatic, and are able to handle salesmen with a macho attitude or who flirt with them. The trainers helped me appreciate that up-counters need to avoid getting enmeshed in long conversations since the job involves paying attention to customers and making sure they quickly signal a salesperson to deal with the person, couple, or family.

On one of the breaks during this session, I asked one of the trainers how many car dealers in California had hired their consulting firm to conduct this kind of training; he told me they could count the number on one hand. I believe the whole approach of making friends and using up-counters was too slow-paced for most dealers in California, where people live a strange lifestyle. While casual on the surface, at the same time, it's always go, go, go.

After I came back from Florida and trained our sales team, we saw sales take a noticeable jump. I knew exactly how many customers we had showing up daily, who was successful, and which salespeople failed to sell many cars and needed to seek employment elsewhere.

Armed with the tools I acquired or refined during training, I was able to obtain this information much more quickly than in the past.

As much as I appreciated the opportunity Sam Linder gave me, after several months, the drive from Los Gatos to Salinas proved too tough. It took at least an hour, and sometimes more, much of it on a two-lane road. After working long hours, navigating the curving route late at night posed a major hazard. Twice I had narrow misses in what could easily have been fatal accidents. At the time, we couldn't find a buyer for our home, and since Sam didn't want to buy it, I told him I would have to give up the job.

However, thanks to what I learned at that training seminar and the principles I then put into practice, I was confident I could make the leap to teaching dealers a similar system to boost their profits. While I never made a major announcement or incorporated business, soon after leaving the Honda dealership in Salinas, I had formed Buzz Howell Automotive, offering sales training for automotive dealers.

Back in Business

Thanks to my years in the industry, I had no problem engaging car dealers, whether in person or on the phone. The first question I always asked: "How many customers do you have coming into your dealership?"

The typical answer: "I have no idea."

"Well, if you hope to increase your sales, the first thing you need to know is how many customers you have," I would tell them. "We'll do a customer count for a week for a decent price, and then you can decide if you want to sign up for our training."

Many of them agreed to the offer. I would send Espe out as my up-counter so they would know how many customers were coming through the doors. The results usually convinced them to hire me. The first dealership we went to was Larry Hopkins Honda in Sunnyvale. It had just lost 30 percent of its sales force after the general manager walked out and took a bunch of their sales staff with him, a common occurrence in the car business.

I talked to Steve Hopkins, now in charge since his father had retired (as many dealers do, Steve left things the same because of name recognition), and explained what I could to help. I offered to train his current staff for a week, and his new sales hires in the second week. Meanwhile, Espe handled customer counts and fact-checked other details, which produced immediate results. By projecting a more professional image and doing better follow-up, sales shot up. Steve couldn't believe how many people were coming into his dealership and the level of increased sales, even with many brand-new personnel. Even old-timers were selling more cars.

Another connection I made while training the staff at Hopkins Honda paid off with additional business. One day on a break, a guy named Mel Price showed up; I knew him from past industry contact. Mel told me that he was working with two guys who were installing a system at the dealership they had field-tested in Southern California with great success. Though quite new and groundbreaking in nature then, some form of it is used now by numerous large dealerships nationwide.

It was called a customer relations room. The company Mel worked for would hire a 90 percent female and 10 percent male staff to answer sales calls from customers. Not only were women more cordial, but they were also better than salesmen (and in those days, most folks in sales were men) who were often tied up or weren't sure how to make appointments. After a dealership spent a great deal of money on advertising to generate these kinds of calls, it could rely on the customer relations department to handle them. A manager, assistant manager, and staff of anywhere from four to twenty-five people answered calls, using headsets and phone scripts that enabled them to handle every call with professionalism. It not only sounded like a great idea, I saw how we could combine it with our training system.

Soon after this, I received a call from Jamie Koph, the owner of Boardwalk Auto Group in Redwood City. After getting an enthusiastic recommendation from Steve

Hopkins, Jamie wanted to talk to me about our training and up-counting processes. We met a few days later. After we explained everything and Jamie reviewed the program with his sales managers, he hired us to start training the following week. Espe hired up-counters who were gathering comprehensive details and information the dealership never had before. In turn, sales increased just as they had at Larry Hopkins Honda. Espe and her staff spent the next two years there; even after she left, Jamie retained her staff.

As I was finishing my training at Boardwalk Auto, Mel Price called me to set up a meeting with the two owners of the company that had installed the customer relations department at Larry Hopkins Honda. They were going to retire and wanted to find people who were talented and honest in interacting with others, especially automotive dealers. Mel had convinced the owners that we could take over their business model from scratch in Northern California. After agreeing to do our best to maintain their excellent reputation, we started a new company, naming it C.A.R.T.T., which was short for Customer Action Results Through Telecommunications.

I know millions of people can't stand telemarketers or the robot nuisance calls that bombard everyone's phones these days. But that's not what we were doing. We simply handled calls from customers who were already interested in our clients' products: cars and trucks. As it turned out, not only did Mel and I make a great team, several of my family members came along for the ride. When you can make a living and have those you love involved with your endeavor, life tastes quite sweet.

CHAPTER 11

A New Adventure

But what does it say? 'The word is near you, in your mouth and in your heart' (that is, the word of faith which we preach): that if you confess with your mouth the Lord Jesus and believe in your heart that God has raised Him from the dead, you will be saved. For with the heart one believes unto righteousness, and with the mouth confession is made unto salvation.

Romans 10:8-10

Once Mel Price and I had agreed on a new business model for Customer Action Results Through Telecommunications, I started making cold calls. That helped me discover that the highest interest for our telephone-call-processing service was in the Sacramento area. Although a 120-mile drive trip from San Jose, with Espe working with me and our children rapidly growing up, we were free to head north. The first customer we signed up was a Chevrolet dealership.

Instead of everyone coming in at once and overwhelming a dealership, we would follow a three-week process for installing a call center. The first week, Espe and I would place an ad in local newspapers announcing, "New Call Center Jobs." We would spend the first three days of the week interviewing fifteen to twenty-five people per day. Then we would call back likely candidates for a second round of interviews Thursday and Friday. That helped narrow the final selection of a manager, assistant manager, and between four and twenty-five telecommunications specialists (depending on the size of the dealership). Now we had a staff eager to start training the following Monday.

Our daughter, Charlene, proved to be a fantastic training manager. A people person, if I ever saw one, she had a knack for making friends throughout her life. Even as a teenager, she had worked for my wholesale car business in the summers. She quickly picked up the finer points of going into dealerships and chatting with used car managers and salespersons to identify older vehicles that weren't moving. Or, find out what trade-ins a particular dealer didn't want on their lots (in those days, domestic dealers like Chevrolet, Ford, and Dodge didn't want imports around for long and vice versa).

After graduating from high school, Charlene came to work for me full time. She proved so adept that I entrusted her with the task of acquiring vehicles over a ten-mile radius northwest of San Jose. In the beginning, she would call me for advice on certain models before closing the deal. Afterward, I would dispatch someone to pick up the car and take it to another dealer or the nearest auto auction. Charlene netted half the profits from these transactions and did so well she soon bought her own car from me—for cash.

Her skills proved quite useful when C.A.R.T.T. needed someone to train call specialists. Charlene set up efficient methods, while her cordial manner quickly created friendships with many of the staff members. She also wrote several phone scripts that specialists could use to handle incoming phone calls, depending on the nature of the inquiry. Her naturally charismatic manner produced great cooperation from the dealerships' managers and staff too.

Once Charlene felt new staffers were ready to process calls professionally, she instructed the dealership's operator to forward all sales calls to the center we had set up in another part of the dealership. In those days, computers and smartphones weren't second nature to even preschoolers. So, we also trained managers how to set up their computer screens with relevant forms and information to track the clients, including their name, address, type of vehicle, and other pertinent information.

During the third week of our rollout, Mel came into the dealership to work with the managers on computer matters, make sure they knew how to replace any specialists who suddenly departed, and oversee the staff to make sure they were staying "on script." In addition, Mel monitored the number of sales calls that had turned into appointments, how many customers showed up, and how many followed through with a vehicle purchase. By the end of that week, he had solid numbers to show sales managers and dealership owners. Looking back later, Mel said those meetings always went smoothly because the staff had started from ground zero but quickly had a comprehensive view of sales inquiries and how to turn prospects into buying customers.

Adding Dealerships

After the Chevrolet dealer, we landed another customer in Sacramento—ironically, a Ford store, one of the auto industry's Big Three and historically a major competitor of Chevrolet. After that, we went to work with a Toyota dealership in Roseville, about twenty miles northeast of Sacramento. After refining operations at those three dealerships and building a solid track record, we had evidence of our effectiveness to show dealers in San Jose and the Oakland-San Francisco Bay Area.

From the outset, one step we decided to take as part of our program was including a one-year follow-up agreement. For a monthly fee, we agreed to conduct monthly, two-day reviews to help ensure dealers' success. This included retraining where needed and offering industry insights to owners and investors. Trying to institute a new program in any business is ripe with the potential for misunderstandings, miscommunications, and other mishaps. So, training is paramount, and knowledge is priceless. We provided both elements, and our follow-up training helped managers and technicians stay on track.

Years later, the brightest memory of those days is how happy and excited dealers, managers, and salespersons were to see us when we returned. The owners in the businesses we served were especially pleased to be able (many for the first time) to see how many customers were calling the dealership each day and what happened when they did.

Once we had returned closer to home, I distributed several dozen packets of material about C.A.R.T.T. and results from the dealerships we had worked with around Sacramento. The first dealership we signed up in metropolitan San Jose was a Nissan dealership in neighboring Santa Clara. The general manager loved anything new and had a sales-oriented mindset. This outlet spilled over to their sales staff and managers, who were excited about the efforts our team made to help them move more vehicles.

Once we had set up operations, the results showed in increased numbers of customers coming to the showroom floor and more sales. After a few weeks, the general manager called me with enthusiastic feedback. He especially liked how he and his sales managers had the exact numbers they needed to improve in their weak areas and remind them when they needed to praise staff members for successfully closing deals.

Soon after this, we completed call center training at a Mitsubishi store and a Dodge dealership in San Jose, Volkswagen in Danville, and a Toyota dealership in Hayward. The following year we received a call from Lone Star Ford in Houston, Texas. After setting an appointment for the following week, Mel and I flew to Houston to see their general manager.

"We need your product," he said when we met. "I was at a Dealer Twenty (an auto industry group) meeting, and one of the Ford dealers made a presentation about it. Our salesmen don't have the time to even take a sales call."

After reaching an agreement, Espe and I flew into Houston on a Sunday night. We found a hotel close to the dealership so we could start early Monday to field incoming calls asking about the job ad and set up times for interviews.

The general manager was obviously telling the truth when he said his salespeople were too busy to answer incoming phone calls. The dealership was closed on Sundays. By the time we arrived at 9:00 a.m. Monday, there were at least thirty customers on the outside lot or the showroom floor. This was a very large dealership, with twenty-five salespersons who came in at nine o'clock and twenty-five more at noon. They had only two overworked operators scrambling to answering incoming calls—100 to 125 a day—with barely enough time to get a name and phone number. We saw that we needed a manager, an assistant, and sixteen specialists.

Texas-Sized Job

Lone Star Ford was by far our company's largest customer to date. That contract would open the doors to others around Houston. That first day we fielded more than one hundred calls and interviewed nearly sixty people. On Tuesday, we answered about 120 calls and interviewed more than seventy-five people. We conducted a second round of interviews on Wednesday and Thursday and hired sixteen employees who understood how to read and work with our telephone scripts.

The two managers we chose were natural leaders and proved proficient at operating our computer software. When Charlene came in the following week for training, she was excited how great the staff absorbed everything she reviewed, not only with our script but their ability to help each other.

When Mel flew in the next week, he called me, excited about the results this team had produced. After his final meeting with the general manager and his staff, he said they were quite thankful that we helped them improve sales so quickly. Now, this may not sound too exciting to someone who isn't in the car business. But what we helped pioneer, along with Mel's former bosses who had launched this system in Southern California, is now in place at more than 75 percent of major dealerships across the United States. Most owners or managers call them customer relations department.

As I mentioned earlier, our contracts included a one-year follow-up obligation, meaning one of us had to fly back to Houston each month. When my turn came to conduct these sessions, it seemed like I had the knack for drawing the short straw. One time a flash flood overwhelmed the street in front of the dealership. Another time, hailstones the size of baseballs walloped the area.

Home Away From Home

Despite such minor setbacks, one of the things Espe and I loved about Houston was attending Sunday services at Lakewood Church, close to two of the dealerships we visited over a two-year period. While we had flown into Houston on a Sunday night the first time, we started arriving by early evening on Saturdays. That way, we could check into a motel and be fully rested before going to Lakewood for services and fellowship prior to starting follow-up training on Monday.

While it was quite a large church, this was before John Osteen's youngest son, Joel, became pastor and grew the congregation into the nation's largest in average Sunday attendance (close to thirty thousand). John was the founding pastor of Lakewood, which opened its doors in 1959 in an old feed store and eventually expanded into a megachurch of more than fifteen thousand members.

We became aware of John Osteen through watching his weekly television program. It aired on numerous Christian TV stations at a time when such shows weren't swamped for attention by hundreds of TV channels, YouTube, and smartphone options that have splintered the modern viewing audience into countless pieces. Not only was Osteen a great communicator, but he also presented his Bible-based messages in a very believable way; the words *honest, trusting,* and *loving* come to mind whenever I reflect on those days. Many others loved his preaching too; as demonstrated by the excitement we could sense pulsating through the auditorium. Many around us lifted their hands, clapped, and called out, "Amen!" or "Praise the Lord!" during praise and worship and the sermons that followed.

One reason we connected so strongly with Osteen was his belief in faith and supernatural healing, something rooted in a dramatic experience he and his wife, Dodie, had with their first daughter. Born with severe health issues that included a broken neck, Lisa faced a bleak future. Doctors said she would never enjoy full physical or mental capabilities—and yet she did after John and Dodie learned about divine healing.

Osteen's emphasis on the faith message especially excited Espe, who had personally observed it and experienced God's power in her daily life. Espe also liked the multicultural flavor of Lakewood, in a time when many churches tended to be of one race or ethnicity. Numerous Mexican and other Spanish-speaking families attended. Many told us they felt uplifted there and like they belonged. Feeling comfortable every time we went, many people welcomed us when we arrived and added, "y'all come back" after services ended. We often returned for evening services.

Expanding the Business

Great restaurants were another enjoyable aspect of our time in Houston. As you can imagine, we both loved Mexican restaurants. Whenever business took us to the suburban city of Spring, we stopped at El Palenque (founded in Houston in 1987 by three brothers, both locations are still going strong). When we preferred steaks or barbecue, we went to the Barbecue Inn in Houston, which opened the year after World War II ended and is still serving up mouth-watering dishes.

However, dining took a back seat to business. On one of my trips back to Houston, I distributed some packets about CARTT that spotlighted the results we had seen at Lone Star Ford. Soon after, we received a call from Gullo-Haas Toyota, one of the top Toyota dealerships in Houston, and signed them up a few weeks later. Espe and I saw results similar to those at Lone Star Ford.

As at Lone Star Ford, the crew quickly absorbed our training and worked quite well with Charlene and Mel. And as with the Ford dealership, the Toyota outlet saw increased sales. Whenever we went back on monthly visits, the sales staff constantly told us how grateful they were when customers came to the dealership ready to buy. Many customers credited the friendly and respectful assistance of telephone staff members who took time to build a relationship with them. Sometimes, after purchasing a vehicle, customers would ask if they could meet their telephone representative in person.

In addition to the Toyota dealership, our work at Lone Star Ford brought an inquiry from a Ford dealer in a small town in northern Oklahoma. However, I had to tell him that he could not handle our typical program; it would cost too much to set up for his size dealership. He was so friendly, though, that we devised a way to launch a center for him by cutting our normal fee in half. We hired a modest-sized staff with only one manager and no assistant. The dealer agreed to pick up Charlene's airfare, hotel, food, and other expenses when she flew in for initial training. Impressed by the group he put together for training, we handled most follow-up matters by telephone. Fortunately, Charlene dodged a tornado during one of her personal visits to Oklahoma.

"Surviving Tornado Alley"

In April of 1993, I was working with dad, helping auto dealers develop customer relations departments. At a small Ford store in Hennessy, Oklahoma, I had to do all the hiring and training.

After landing in Oklahoma City, I took a taxi to a hotel. The next morning the dealership's office manager picked me up for the seventy-five-minute drive to Hennessy. Throughout the trip, I grilled her with questions about tornado preparations, although she assured me it was too early in the year.

"Besides, you live in California," she said. "You have to know what to do during an earthquake."

Still, since I would be there for a week, I wanted to know just in case. Looking out the dealership's window after we arrived, I saw nothing in front of me, a Pizza Hut to the right, a Sonic to the left, and not much else. I smiled broadly when I made it to my hotel that night in a much larger city.

After dinner, I enjoyed watching mall walkers before going back to my below-ground lodgings; the hotel clerk had granted my request for the safest room possible. That night I awoke to a raucous noise. Flipping on the TV, I saw a funnel cloud—close to me! I dove into the bathtub (I had seen that in a movie) and cried and prayed all night.

The next morning, I awoke to snow covering my loaner car and all the roads. To everyone's surprise at the dealership, I made it. The work ethic dad instilled in me demanded I go. After a rocky start, I loved the rest of the week and everyone I met.

—*Charlene Allnutt, Daughter*

The Best Advertising

This kind of agreement, and others, started to generate some excellent word-of-mouth advertising, which is the most valuable kind. Along the way, I even received a call from Sam Linder, who I had worked for earlier in Salinas before the 120-mile roundtrip commute got to be too much. Sam invited us to speak about our telecommunications business at his Dealer Twenty Group meeting in Denver, Colorado. Sponsored by the National Independent Auto Dealers Association, these networking groups meet across North America, helping dealer-owners and managers become more profitable.

Sam gave us an hour to discuss our ideas and the outlook for the future of customer relations. Many attendees asked questions, including one who asked us to call him later. He was part of Bill Pierre Ford, a family-owned dealership in Seattle. Founded in 1947, they had a long-standing reputation in the community, and he wanted to make sure we wouldn't do anything to tarnish their image. We assured him we would only hire a staff that would honor their status, even offering sales managers the chance to sit in on the hiring interviews.

Given Seattle's reputation for rain nearly every other day of the year, when Espe and I showed up at Pierre Ford, we were pleased to be greeted by a sunny, beautiful day instead of overcast skies. However, instead of telephones ringing off the hook as they usually did, we only received a few calls. Finally, I asked the owner what was going on; he replied, "great weather happens very seldom, so when it does, people tend to enjoy the day." Fortunately, on Tuesday, the phones started ringing.

After setting up that call center, we flew to Tucson, Arizona, where we had signed up for O'Reilly Chevrolet. In business twenty-six years longer than the Ford dealership in Seattle, this was the oldest dealership we had under contract. (The only one older than O'Reilly's was a place in Southern California I worked for in my early days in the car business, and it's no longer around.) These two dealerships' longevity impressed me because in the auto business, change is constant. Those who don't go out of business often sell their dealership to someone else. Yet, years later, both are still around.

When Espe and I started interviewing people on Monday, we were treated like family by the third generation of O'Reillys. Our success proved nearly identical to what happened in Seattle. And as in Houston, two of the things we enjoyed about Tucson were the friendliness of the people and the great restaurants.

Another Move

Because of our regular travels, after we landed some business in Southern California, we finally decided to put our home in San Jose on the market and relocate. We found an apartment in Huntington Beach, about thirty-five miles south of Los Angeles. Only about a mile from the beach, when we weren't tied up with business, we loved to take a quick getaway to the Pacific Ocean. Having lived there in the past, we had experienced the area's breathtaking scenery and rolling ocean waves. It's no wonder millions want to live there.

The first place we worked at in the Los Angeles area was a Mercedes dealer in Beverly Hills. Ironically, the general manager who had hired us got fired by the time Espe and I arrived at the dealership. After explaining our system and showing tangible evidence of the results other dealers had experienced, the new general manager agreed to install our program. The advertisements we placed in area newspapers attracted the best-educated and most knowledgeable people we had ever seen. When Charlene came the following week to conduct training, she told us it was her best, most productive experience ever. Mel showed similar excitement, and when he showed the results for the previous week to the general manager, the smile that crossed his face could have lit up Hollywood Boulevard.

After that, we worked with a Toyota dealership in Ontario, about thirty-five miles east of Los Angeles. A bustling dealership that made a considerable amount of new car sales, we had to hire two managers and twenty specialists to handle the call volume. As in Beverly Hills, the advertisement in the Ontario newspaper worked extremely well. The managers were excited because they couldn't believe how many calls they were receiving, thanks to more professional methods of handling them.

While we were in Orange County one day, Espe and I made an appointment with the general manager of a Toyota dealership in Westminster to set up a deal apart from C.A.R.T.T. We could tell it was running out of steam. While Mel had moved to Southern California too, we could see his interest in the business waning. Plus, I think as dealers recognized what a great idea we had, they decided to set up their own call centers without the expense of paying outside consultants.

The owner's daughter was gradually taking over the Toyota dealership from her father and needed some help with day-to-day basics. Initially, she agreed to hire Espe to handle the up-counting of their incoming customers. Once Espe provided her with some daily and weekly numbers of customers and results, the owner's daughter recognized she had a huge problem—they weren't converting "window shoppers" into buying customers.

Espe then set up a meeting where I explained how they could raise sales. Seeing the need for sales training and pointers on running the dealership more efficiently, she hired me on a ninety-day retainer. When their car sales increased by 50 percent, she hired me for another ninety days.

Brush with Fame

Right after I signed the second contract, I had another brush with fame, a bit like the day in 1972 when I saw Steve Wozniak walk through the dealership in San Jose. On June 17, 1994, the television set in the customer lounge at the Toyota dealership carried a prominent story all morning and into the afternoon: live video of O.J. Simpson sitting in the back of his Ford Bronco while a friend drove his SUV down the freeway. A stream of police cars flowed behind the Bronco.

At this time, O.J. was the subject of constant, nationwide news coverage after the murder five days earlier of his wife, Nicole Brown Simpson, and Ronald Goldman. We were only three blocks from a 405 Freeway overpass, which we crossed daily en route to the dealership. When they announced where this pursuit was taking place, we realized this strange motorcade would likely pass by on the freeway before too much longer. Espe talked another person into taking her place counting customers, and we drove a few blocks down the street to find a viewing spot on the overpass.

When we arrived, it was obvious hundreds of other people had the same plan. Fortunately, we secured a good vantage point. By the time O.J.'s vehicle came into view, the overpass was filled with a sea of humanity, with many in the crowd yelling out shouts of support for O.J. We could see him coasting down the 405 Freeway, normally congested with thousands of vehicles but now barren of other traffic. In retrospect, it seems eerie and surreal, as if it almost never happened. The Bronco meandered down the highway at what looked like about ten miles an hour, sometimes going back and forth in the lane. About twenty highway patrol cars or more were behind them. When they got near the overpass where we were standing, O.J. put his head out the window and waved to the cheering crowd.

Ironically, we now live in Las Vegas, where O.J. ultimately settled after his release from prison after serving nearly nine years for a robbery conviction. While he has told news reporters that life is fine now, I pray he comes to know the truth of John 3:16.

While it was interesting being part of a scene that attracted the attention of the entire country, before long, our time at the Toyota dealership suddenly ended. Although the owner's daughter appreciated our efforts and regularly complimented us on the results, her father blew his stack over the cost. With fifteen days left on my second contract, he complained so strenuously that she paid me for the last two weeks, and we quietly departed. As with other separations in the auto business, I left with no hard feelings.

Besides, a few days later, I would again see the Lord provide in our time of need. After getting our phone number from Charlene, my old boss Sam Linder called with an offer I couldn't refuse. After paying our rent through the end of the month so we would leave on good terms with the landlord, we headed back north. We were about to discover the thrill of living close to Charlene, her husband, Frank, and our grandchildren—not far from the Pacific Ocean. I was about to become part-owner of a Cadillac and Honda dealership.

CHAPTER 12

Offer of a Lifetime

But let all those rejoice who put their trust in You;
let them ever shout for joy, because You defend
them; let those also who love Your name be joyful
in You. For You, O LORD, will bless the righteous;
with favor You will surround him as with a shield.

Psalm 5:11-12

One reason I feel so confident that the Lord is always looking out for us is the timing of Sam Linder's call, coming right after my relationship with the Toyota dealership in Westminster soured. When I spent several months working for his dealership in Salinas in 1990, I never dreamed that four years later, he would offer me the chance to become a part-owner of the operation.

As I mentioned in chapter ten, the reason I stopped working for him previously was the long and sometimes treacherous daily drive between Salinas and Los Gatos. But when we made the decision to move back to Northern California, our apartment in Pacific Grove was just a scenic, twenty-mile drive from San Linder Cadillac-Honda. Considering the stress and narrow misses four years earlier, I loved living so close. Finding an apartment next to Charlene, Frank, and two of our granddaughters put the icing on the cake. Frank would join me at Sam Linder Cadillac-Honda as a team leader; most days, we rode to work together.

Once Sam and I had an agreement on paper, I hired Mark, as one of our sales managers and our used truck buyer. As a team leader of five to seven sales associates, Frank would train them in selling vehicles after I did some initial training on the basic steps in dealing with prospective buyers. Both Mark and Frank had been working for a Ford dealer in the nearby town of Seaside and jumped at the opportunity to join my team.

After my departure in 1990, Sam had had five different general managers operating his dealership. That high rate of turnover gives an indication of how successful they had been. Sam was pleased about my plans to bring two auto industry veterans aboard as part of the sales team. Mark and Frank were sharp and good at their trade. Not only did other salespeople like Frank's positive attitude when it came time to make a sale, but Frank was also a great closer. Customers liked his British accent too.

In a short time, the dealership had climbed out of the red and was showing a profit. One of the promotions we used involved special sales twice a year at the huge Northridge Mall, about a half-mile from the dealership. Our first took place over Memorial Day weekend of 1995. After four days of hard work, the dealership saw its best mall sales ever. We made another sale at Northridge over Labor Day weekend in early September, with similar success.

Lifted Up...and Up

The following year Sam Linder came up with an attention-getting promotion called "Sale in the Sky." It involved bringing in a giant crane to lift a conversion van—fully equipped with a bed, cooking stove, seating area, and bathroom—into the sky. When hoisted up, the van sat more than four stories off the ground. That may not seem so high until factoring in the van swaying in the winds of the Pacific Ocean, a frequent occurrence during the summer in Salinas. Plus, during the early morning hours, thick ocean fog often rolled inland. Mark volunteered to go up in the van and sit suspended in the sky from Friday through Sunday. For our first sky sale, we set a goal of selling forty cars (new or used) in order to get Mark down. We hit the mark by 6:00 p.m. on Sunday.

"How do you feel?" I asked Mark when he was back safely on the ground.

"Great," he replied. "I'm confident about doing this next year."

Because of the hefty expenses involved in putting on this kind of sale, next year we increased the weekend's goal to fifty cars. But when six o'clock arrived that Sunday, we were still seven cars short. Someone on the lot hatched the idea to call a popular radio station DJ and ask him to announce an "emergency." If we didn't sell seven more cars, poor Mark would be stranded in midair! Sensing an opportunity to get the radio station some publicity at the same time he helped us out, the disk jockey played it up. Throughout the evening, he kept reminding listeners of the emergency. It worked. One by one, those who heard him steadily showed up on the lot.

Even so, it took a last-hour move to bring in the final buyer. Our son Albert had been working for the dealership that summer to earn money to go back to Harvard Divinity School. He had called a friend in San Jose to alert him to Uncle Mark's plight. Albert's friend made the hour-long drive to Salinas and bought car number fifty, closing the deal at 1:00 a.m. on Monday.

When Mark reached the ground, though, his face looked ashen. His legs and arms were trembling. Nervous about the whole thing, he imitated boxer Roberto Duran II in 1980. Duran was the middleweight boxer who bowed out of a championship fight with Sugar Ray

Leonard by lifting his arms and saying, "no más, no más" (no more). After his "no más," Mark never went back into the wild blue yonder again.

Making Friends

During our first year in the area, we lived close to Charlene and Frank in Pacific Grove and went to church in that area. However, once we decided to move to a home just three miles from the dealership, we joined Victory Outreach Church. A vibrant, energetic leader named Herb Valero had taken over as pastor in 1989. Originally from the Los Angeles area, Herb had a major drug problem. Victory Outreach—which started as a single church in Los Angeles and gradually expanded into a worldwide ministry network—helped him kick the habit. Soon after getting sober, Herb started spiritual training for ministry. After getting some experience in San Jose, he accepted a call from the church in Salinas.

Pastor Herb and I became quite friendly. Victory Outreach's ministry included a halfway house for men coming out of prison; that home was located next to our dealership. Having worked with Tony Ortiz (mentioned in chapter eight) and his Breakout Prison Outreach in San Jose, I was comfortable associating with men who had been through rough patches in life. Likewise, Pastor Herb felt quite comfortable with my faith and at times asked me to deliver the Sunday message if he was out of town. Several times, Herb's wife, Margo, invited Espe to the church's large women's group to preach on faith. It's quite a gift, one that animates Espe's voice and actions whenever she speaks about it.

One of the special memories I have of Pastor Herb is his heart for the lost souls of this world. I witnessed this love in action many times. That is why Espe and I were so blessed when we could later attend a twentieth-anniversary banquet celebrating his time in ministry, held in the beautiful city of Monterey on April 5, 2010.

Another time, we attended a statewide Victory Outreach convention in Southern California, where we met people with an infectious enthusiasm for evangelism. The convention speakers included the noted pastor John Hagee, founder of Cornerstone Church in San Antonio, Texas. Hagee inspired everyone with his call to be active in our love for others, bold in our faith, and to be concerned for their welfare and eternal destiny if they failed to accept Jesus as their Savior.

Not only did Herb and Margo became close friends, but Espe also hired their outgoing and friendly daughter, Darlene, to do up-counting of customers at Sam Linder's. We last saw Herb and Margo in 2016 when they came to Las Vegas for a mini-vacation to visit us and a pastor-friend at a Victory Outreach church here.

About a year later, I heard about his tragic death. On March 14, 2017, while praying outside his home with a parishioner, the man fatally stabbed Herb in the neck. When we heard about the news, Espe and I felt like we had been hit with a sledgehammer. Fortunately, we have the very real hope of a future reunion with Herb in heaven. As you read in chapter 1, I have already been there and know it's a real place.

Subdued Success

When I took over as general manager at Sam Linder's, the dealership had a great sales manager, Jim. He helped me a lot, particularly by supporting my efforts to improve sales and profitability of all the departments. Another key person was the finance manager, Bill, who worked closely with Mark and put together some creative financing deals through our bank and finance companies. I gave Bill numerous high fives for the deals he put together that, at first glance, seemed impossible. The sales department had some good salespersons, and with several additions that really took a liking to our training, along with Frank's help as a team leader, we saw a noticeable increase in sales and profits.

By boosting new and used car sales, we created more revenue through what is known in the industry as service and parts departments. New vehicles have to undergo a pre-delivery inspection before sale, with checks of such things as battery, hoses, brakes, lights, assorted fluid levels, lubricating locks, latches, and hinges. A technician also inspects a used vehicle for any flaws and gets it mechanically ready for the eventual owner. Parts come into play when they need repairs, either before or after the sale.

"Dream of a Lifetime"

When Charlene and I married, I never dreamed that one day I would be working alongside her father. Thanks to Buzz's expert sales skills and teaching ability, I became a success. It started with helping Buzz moving cars from place to place or lot to lot, retrieving titles, or whatever else he asked me to do. I was learning the industry from the ground up.

One day Buzz suggested I talk to a customer on the lot. I didn't want to, but he encouraged me to just simply go and see what the guy wanted. I figured there was no harm in having a conversation. As we talked, he asked if he could take a test drive. I went to the office and grabbed the keys.

During that test drive, the guy fell in love with the car. Now, Buzz had already told me when we returned to park in front of the office. As soon as we did, Buzz told me to have the guy fill out an application. An hour later, the customer drove off in his new car. Right after he left, Buzz informed me I had just made three hundred dollars! I thought he was joking; that was the easiest money I had ever earned. That's also when I caught the bug.

Over the years, we worked in many dealerships together. The longest period was at Sam Linder Cadillac-Honda in Salinas, when Buzz, several family members, and I went into the dealership and turned it around to profitability.

Buzz called us "The Dream Team," but because of his positive attitude and leadership, we became "The Reality Team." Thanks to Buzz, I enjoyed a twenty-five-year-long career in the automotive industry and made a comfortable living for my family.

—*Frank Allnutt, Son-in-law*

New car sales also mean more warranty service for three to five years. Service is also needed for used vehicles to get them ready for sale, along with components like tires and a long list of other parts—before and after the sale. Another area where we helped Linder become more profitable was in the finance department; we sold more service warranties on new and used vehicles and various insurance products.

Previously, I talked about the value of tracking the number of customers who come into a dealership. (I still have complete records from 1998 to 2002, so anyone can understand the results.) We could see the difference by 2000; Sam Linder had seen five consecutive years of increased profitability and growth in sales of new Cadillacs, Hondas, and used cars. Thanks to this success and my ownership bonuses, I was eventually able to purchase a 25 percent interest in the dealership.

One of the Dealer Twenty Honda Group members that Espe and I were with at a Honda yearly meeting that I attended for Sam Linder was in Las Vegas, which is kind of ironic because we ended up living there at the end of 2007. Espe and I wound up becoming good friends with that couple, Lou and Debbie.

Lou and Debbie with Wayne Newton. Wayne and Debbie are from the same Native American Powhatan Tribe. Debbie is a direct descendent of Pocahontas and one of the likenesses they used in the animated movie.

However, something happened that tempered my excitement about these business achievements. It came in the form of a call in 1999 from my brother, Billy. He was staying with mom in the same small home in San Jose that we had moved into in the late 1950s.

"Mom's having major memory problems," he said before pausing as he momentarily choked up. "She's forgetting a lot. Major things."

Many people know what it's like dealing with aging parents or other family members, but there was an added layer of complexity since our mother had her finger in a lot of pies. Her assets included inheritances that included several family-owned farms in Nebraska, Kansas, and Missouri. Soon after Billy's call, the manager at one of the farms in Nebraska called, saying it was high time for me to start overseeing things.

Naturally, soon after that, I drove into San Jose to see how Mom was doing. Fighting back with her characteristic stubbornness, she insisted: "I'm fine." Not convinced, I went to see an attorney at a law firm in Salinas. He promised to help me when the time came.

A few months later, Mom showed up for a hearing at the courthouse in San Jose, accompanied by an attorney who looked like he was in his eighties too. During closing statements, he advised my mother and the judge that it would be best if I took over all the affairs of the farms and responsibility for her assets.

Family Matters

After the court hearing, our first move was to place all mom's holdings into H&G Farms. The H was for Howell, which came from brothers Basil, William, and Wade, and the G from our youngest brother, Jerre Gilliam (and our mother). Each party held a 20 percent ownership interest in the corporation. As the oldest, I became president; everyone agreed to Charlene serving as secretary. The setup required holding regular board meetings. As president, I was responsible for all the agendas and reports. Since Wade lived in upstate New York, most of the time, we met by telephone.

However, one time we all traveled to Nebraska and met up in Rulo, where mom first lived after dad enlisted in the military during World War II. We held one meeting at the Stephenson Hotel in Falls City. This was a great time for my mother and many people who knew her from decades earlier. Mom's old friends, many of whom had also known her sisters before she moved to San Jose, were overjoyed to see her and all us boys. The farm manager took us to see the Cunningham Farms in all three states. Everyone was blown away to see how many acres we owned and how nice everyone was to us.

A few years later, we mixed business with a historic family occasion: Albert's graduation from Harvard Divinity School in 2002. We planned the quarterly board meeting of H&G Farms to coincide with our trip to Boston. That required us to stay in Boston for an extra day to meet with Bill and Wade. Although Jerre couldn't make it, we still had a quorum for our morning meeting at a hotel.

This sojourn came six years after Espe visited Boston on her own to celebrate the birth of Albert's first son, Wisdom, on February 16, 1996. Espe arrived a day after the infant's birth.

Graduation Day

We couldn't wait to fly to Boston to watch Albert walk across the stage to receive his diploma. Held on campus, the ceremony attracted a huge crowd. Hosts and hostesses handed out souvenir lunch containers imprinted with "Harvard Divinity School" on the front and food and snacks inside. We sat outside on folding chairs with a canopy over us in case of rain—which it did.

Once everyone was in place, the music started, graduates marched in dressed in their caps and gowns. In a millisecond, we could hear the clicking of cameras and see flashes of light as the "aahs" grew louder, and everyone started applauding. While the speakers inspired us, Espe and I couldn't wait for them to call out "Albert Howell." Our hearts burst with joy over his accomplishment. Everyone else felt the same way about their students. You could feel the love and happiness pulsating through the audience.

Afterward, we walked around campus to snap photos and enjoy the beauty of the historic, ivy-covered buildings and legendary Harvard Square. The latter functions as a commercial center for Harvard students, residents of the western section of Cambridge, and the western and northern suburbs of Boston. Established in 1636, Harvard is the oldest institution of higher education in the United States.

In the afternoon, we toured downtown Boston with Espe's mother, Espe's sister; our daughter, Charlene; our son, Gavin; and our grandsons, Wisdom and

Zakerey and granddaughter Frankey. Albert served as our tour guide. We walked on the route Paul Revere followed when he famously warned of the British army's advance and saw Park Street Church, Faneuil Hall, Copley Square, Old State House, and Beacon Hill. We ended our tour at Boston Public Garden. America's first public garden, it has six hundred varieties of trees and an ever-changing array of flowers. It is famous for its Swan Boats, a fleet of pontoon pleasure boats that have been around since 1877. They cruise around a four-acre lake that contains numerous ducks and swans.

That night we stopped for dinner at TGI Fridays. Packed to the gills, we waited for what seemed like an eternity to order. An hour later, Espe got so mad she stalked back to the kitchen. Soon, she returned with ten people trailing behind her, arms loaded with food plates. Our group started clapping.

New York, New York

The year after our trip to Boston, bother Wade married a wonderful woman named Joyce in Rochester, New York. Espe, Espe's mother, son Gavin, and I all went. Esperanza Senior was thrilled over the opportunity to finally see New York City, which we planned to do after the wedding.

We arrived in Rochester a day early so we could see nearby Niagara Falls, which straddles the border with

Canada. The drive took about two hours; when you pass the border checkpoint, you can see and hear the falls' roaring power as the water crashes down the falls into Canada before flowing into Lake Ontario. Once we parked our vehicle and went to the observation area, we marveled as we watched the incredible power of so much water cascading down Horseshoe Falls with 2,509 tons of force. It was truly a wonder to behold.

We also took the Maid of the Mist boat tour on the lake next to the falls. Although the double-decker boat can accommodate numerous tour groups, next to the trio of 170-feet-high falls (Horseshoe, Bridal Veil, and American) that make up Niagara Falls, we feel small indeed. The ride gave everyone a firsthand feel of the power of the water. True to the name of the boat, mist-covered everyone in the boat. It's no wonder they gave us all a raincoat before we set out for the ride.

Despite the great weather on the day of our trip to the falls, August brings regular rain alerts to Rochester. So, any outdoor event calls for a large tent, such as the one erected the next day for the wedding ceremony and the reception. God blessed our family that day; the rain held off until the evening. More than seventy-five guests came to witness and celebrate with Wade and Joyce: Joyce's daughter, Adrienne, her bridesmaid; her sons, Matt and Jordon; and Wade's sons, Eric and Jamie—both held the title of best man.

When they came into the ceremony area, everyone looked very happy, and Joyce looked radiant in her beautiful dress. The minister and I were there at the altar. After I gave a word about marriage from the Bible, the minister led them in their vows. After the ceremony, everyone went outside the tent to join hands in a circle as the DJ played "Will the Circle be Unbroken."

After an early dinner, the DJ started the music. Everyone had a great time, with Espe's mother beaming as she danced with Wade to the Paul Simon tune "Late in The Evening."

The next day we drove down to New York City. As we reached the skyline, my mother-in-law broke out into a grin and stayed that way until we arrived at the Marriott Hotel on Broadway, just a minute from Times Square. The next day we went to the Statue of Liberty, stopping to see adjoining Ellis Island, the historical place where twelve million immigrants were processed from 1892 to 1954. We especially enjoyed the boat trip out to the island since the guide included plenty of background and history in his presentation.

That night I was able to get tickets for the revival of *42nd Street*, the musical comedy classic that was based on the 1933 movie (Espe's mother had seen the film as a teenager). The next day we did tours of the Empire State Building, Times Square, and Broadway. That called for a lot of walking and an umbrella to protect my mother-in-law from the rain. Despite the weather, to make Esperanza Senior's lifelong dream of a trip to New York was one of the highlights of our trip.

Bowing Out

Turns out, 2003 also marked my final year with Sam Linder's dealership. I had expected to eventually become a majority owner of the business, but we couldn't come to an agreement. I told him after the Memorial Day mall sale that I didn't want to hang around. He tried to talk me out of leaving, but when that didn't work, he convinced me to stay for six months longer so he could find the right person to take my place. I agreed since I didn't have any bad feelings toward Sam. In fact, this opportunity had been one of the best in my varied career.

However, if I had to identify the key reason for my departure, I credit that to the Lord's leading. One day, as I moved around a few cars on the used car lot to arrange the right color display, I sensed the Holy Spirit whispering in His soft voice, warning that if I stayed around the dealership, I wouldn't be alive much longer. That sent me to heart and vascular specialists in Salinas and Monterey. While both gave me "perfect health" reports initially, I sensed this battle wasn't over.

CHAPTER 13

A Blessing from God

Behold, children are a heritage from the LORD,
the fruit of the womb is a reward. Like arrows in
the hand of a warrior, so are the children of one's
youth. Happy is the man who has his quiver full of
them; they shall not be ashamed.

Psalm 127:3-5

With my departure from Sam Linder at the end of 2003, it was time to slow down and spend more time with my family, especially Espe's mother, who had been widowed in January of 2000. Naturally, Esperanza Senior and my wife were much closer to Alberto Jiménez Aldape than me, but I grieved his passing and wanted to support my mother-in-law. She had lost the husband who had risked everything to bring his family the kind of life that for many remains an elusive dream.

Espe's father was born in Boquillas del Carmen, a small Mexican mining village near the Texas border. Tragically, his father died in an accident in the mines when Alberto was just six years old. Stunned, his mother decided to move with her four young children to Piedras Negras, today a city of 150,000 but much smaller back then. As the oldest child, after Alberto started school, he also found a job shining shoes to help earn money to support the family. As a teenager and young man, Alberto worked in a grocery store, including driving a truck to deliver food to ranches in the area.

As the years progressed, Alberto and his mother bought a small grocery store in town. Espe's mother (and namesake), Esperanza Troncoso, always shopped at the Aldapes' grocery because they stocked the finest food and produce in the area. After Esperanza had shopped at their store for two years, one day, two of Alberto's family members came to see her parents. Wearing serious looks, they told Esperanza's parents that thirty-one-year-old Alberto wanted to marry their oldest daughter, who had just turned eighteen. Her father, Enrique Troncoso, gave his permission; he knew Alberto personally and that he was an honest, hardworking man. Enrique granted them permission to get married the following week. Such events were common in Mexico in 1944.

Children would soon follow: my future wife, Esperanza Junior, was born on August 1, 1945, and Emma Hilda on November 5, 1946. However, heartbreak followed a few years later with the death of Alberto's mother. After losing his father at such a young age, Alberto had been extremely close to his mother. The ensuing grief that consumed his life left Alberto distraught and unable to work. Although his wife tried to maintain the grocery store in his absence, it floundered.

Finally, they left Mexico for Texas in December of 1953, settling in Corpus Christi, where Alberto had a job with a cement company waiting for him. Espe doesn't remember much about those days, except for the grind of attending school. Speaking only Spanish held her back, and she had to repeat her first-grade year.

Go West, Young Man

Texas didn't bring the success Alberto had hoped to achieve. In 1956 the family hopped a train from Corpus Christi to Pasadena, California, where they stayed with Espe's Uncle Sam. Successful in the acting business, Sam had moved into a mansion that could easily accommodate them. With roles at the Pasadena Playhouse and under the bright lights in Hollywood, he had acted in nine-stage productions and four TV shows. During his early days, Sam attended an acting academy where he met famed actor George Reeves, who went on to play Superman in the TV series, and a young up-and-comer named Dustin Hoffman.

Not too long after buying his spacious home in Pasadena, Sam's parents; most of his brothers and sisters; and Albert, Esperanza, and their three girls were all living under his roof.

Thanks to extensive family connections, within a few months, Enrique Troncoso helped Alberto and his brothers, Jose and Jesus, find jobs at a glass company in Covina. Espe still remembers the parties and lunches Sam hosted, which is how she had the chance to meet George Reeves.

Espe's family would live with Uncle Sam for a year before Alberto saved enough money to rent a home in South Los Angeles for two more years. Meanwhile, he saved every penny possible toward a down payment on a home in Azusa. Because houses didn't cost a small fortune in the early 1960s, in those twenty-four months, the family eventually had enough money to buy a modest-sized place. Despite the move, their family ties remained strong. Esperanza Senior's younger brother, Enrique, and his wife, Celsa, also lived in Azusa. Alberto and his family attended—and had at their home—parties well-attended by aunts, uncles, brothers, sisters, grandparents, cousins, and friends. They also celebrated birthdays or holiday events at the lake or ocean.

Alberto and Esperanza raised Espe in an atmosphere of love. During summers in high school, Espe worked at a nursery. After graduation, she continued working part-time and got a side job at La Tolteca, the Mexican restaurant where we met. Her great personality, infectious laugh, and good looks caught my eye. She seemed like she lived an exciting life. When Espe agreed to go on a date with me, I could barely wait for the day to arrive.

I first met Alberto and Esperanza on February 2, 1966, at their home. They asked me a few questions, using Espe to translate. As time passed, I could tell Esperanza Senior was really the boss of the family. A good-natured man, Alberto was incredibly kind and loving toward his wife and their four children. He was a good provider and always friendly to me. As I mentioned in chapter 4, they gave us their blessing when we told them we wanted to get married in Las Vegas. Later, after they moved to San Jose to live with us, we would spend the next thirty-three years together, with the exception of a four-year period when they stayed with relatives.

When they lived with us in Salinas, they thoroughly enjoyed their time with their great-granddaughters, Chezaraye and Frankey, and great-grandsons, Zakerey and Wisdom, who were close in age (Wisdom is Albert's son; the other three are Charlene and Frank's children). Everyone who has been a grandparent or great-grandparent knows the specialness of watching little ones who will one day take our place.

Family Heritage

The rich family heritage Espe and I enjoy should give you an idea of why family is so important in our lives. The love we had for our four children blossomed more fully as grandchildren began to arrive in March of 1988. First came Chezaraye, Charlene and Frank's oldest daughter. They then welcomed Frankey in 1990 and Zakerey in 1996. My oldest daughter, Coralee, and her husband, James, gave life to Sarah in September of 1988; Rachel, a year later; and Elizabeth (Lisa) in October of 1994. Wisdom was born in February of 1996 to son Albert and his wife, Diana.

Then came great-grandchildren: Peyton in 2009, Jacob in 2011, Mariah in 2013, Azalea in 2018, and Scarlett in 2021. After a while, it gets hard to trace all the branches of the family tree, but suffice it to say, they helped create lasting memories. Among them are great birthday parties, joyous weddings, trips to balloon festivals in New Mexico, and high school and college graduations. Then there were Christmas trips to Disneyland with Charlene's and Coralee's families and hunts for Beanie Babies with Chezaraye and Frankey as far away as San Francisco, Sonora, and Sacramento. We also enjoyed the chance to relax at a good movie or take a trip to Giants Stadium in San Francisco to see Barry Bonds smash home runs (before we knew he was "on the juice"). In 2001 we also bought a timeshare in Newport Beach; our family always looks forward to our summer week of relaxation at the pool or on the beach.

Wisdom Howell
University of San Francisco Law School

"A Lighthouse"

My grandfather—or Pop, as I have always called him—has been the guiding light of my turbulent life, like a steadying force on an ever-rocky sea. Whenever something is out of place, I can look to him for guidance. His influence helped me graduate from UNLV's Journalism and Media Studies program as a two-time member of the dean's list. His wisdom (pun intended) also steered me toward pursuing a career in law, which is how I wound up a student at the University of San Francisco's law school.

Pop's ability to shine an effervescent light on any dark or eerie situation stems from his deeply rooted understanding of reality. His rocky path in life has given him the requisite tools to approach any situation with a clear mind and reasonable approach. I made it a point to mimic Pop's unique ability to maintain control. This approach has undergirded my persevering attitude.

To understand the mechanics of this blue-collared Nebraskan, I spent my formative years looking to the source of Pop's light. I always wondered how every person he interacted with lit up like a tree on Christmas, whether a gas station attendant, waitress, usher, gardener, pool cleaner, or neighbor. Everyone who came into contact with Pop left with a smile.

I took special notice of his mannerisms and tone of voice. No matter the creed, color, class, or nationality, Pop approached each person with the same vibrant energy, full eye contact, and undivided attention. He made sure each moment belonged to the other person. This realization changed my life and view of the world. It made me realize that while society tells us to build artificial walls between our neighbors, in reality, we are all one. I have Pop to thank for that. Well, that and my corny sense of humor. I guess that must be a Nebraska thing.

—*Wisdom Howell, Grandson*

Retirement also gave me time to do things like fixing up my mother's home in San Jose. Billy, mom, and I also made the trip to Nebraska I mentioned in chapter twelve for the H&G board meeting and to tour the family farms. Prior to that, our previous visit to Falls City had been for the funeral of mom's oldest sister, Mary.

This trip was a much brighter one and included giving my brothers a chance to see Rulo, Falls City, and the farms for the first time. However, mom was sad to see the population declines in the Great Plains. When we left Rulo for San Jose in 1945, the town had more than seven hundred people. Over the next six decades, it had dwindled below one hundred. Falls City's population of around fifteen thousand in 1945 had shrunk to about forty-five hundred.

Our farm manager, Rick Barnes, picked us up in his four-door pickup truck to show us the farms. We were all surprised by how much knowledge he had of their size and boundaries and the area's history. Later, he told us he owned an airplane and could take us up for an aerial view, but we passed on that offer.

As we walked around Rulo, we went to see the family homestead where mom grew up. Inside, mom was shocked by its deterioration. We also drove by the Catholic church she used to attend and ended up at the resting place of her grandparents, father, mother, and two sisters. We then crossed over the Rulo bridge to the farms in Missouri and later to the farms in nearby Kansas. As we walked around, Rick told us how much each farm was able to produce and how happy he was with our farmers.

Some of the farms had small lakes and rivers, which mom remembered getting dammed up by beavers, causing flooding on the farms. I was surprised to see the beauty of the trees and foliage, as well as the stream-like quality of what (from mom's past descriptions) I had assumed, were raging rivers.

On the way back to Rulo, mom wanted to stop in town to talk with residents; she found quite a few who remembered her family (after our corporate board meeting the next day, she encountered others who knew them). Reliving the past pleased mom so much she offered to buy us a late lunch at the restaurant on the river. On the way back past her family's home, she mentioned how the house across the street had been a hideout for legendary bank robber Jesse James after some of his stickups.

Special Experience

As we chatted during lunch, we could see how happy mom was, which made everyone delighted to be a part of this once-in-a-lifetime experience. The next morning after breakfast, we met with mom's attorney. The firm's office was just a few blocks from the hotel. The attorney covered everything pertinent to the estate and the farms and advised us on how to organize everything in the future.

After the meeting and lunch, we took a trip to an Indian reservation located about fifteen miles from Rulo. My mom had pleasant childhood memories of playing with the kids who lived there. While we couldn't find the playground where she and the other kids had run and laughed together, there was no missing the casino that had sprouted amid the cornfields. Jerre and Billy enjoyed drinks and played the slot machines, while Wade and I just watched our mom throw away twenty dollars in the one-eyed bandits. After several hours, we left.

With nightfall closing in, I took over the driving and soon spotted a car behind me, following much too close. If I sped up, so did he. This bothered Billy and Jerre, a hot-blooded pair who wanted me to pull over and get ready to fight the tailgater. Instead, I sped up and made it into Falls City. When I saw a cop car, I pulled over and parked next to the cruiser. The other car drove away. My mother commented: "It must have been the Cadillac we were driving. People from around here do not buy expensive cars."

We left the next morning to fly back home. When we arrived back in San Jose and went to mom's home, the difference before and after our trip was like night and day. While we were in Nebraska, two men from Victory Outreach Ministries had set about cleaning up, painting, removing old carpet, and freshening up the house, which we were preparing to put on the market. They performed a miracle, making it look so different and quite livable, almost ready to go up for sale.

"Golden Treasures"

During my childhood, I was quite fortunate to grow up with my maternal grandparents living around the corner—close enough that my sister and I were able to pack up our bags and "run away" from our chores.

Nanny and Pop always welcomed us with love, hugs, and boisterous laughter. Even after more than fifty years together, they have taught us that love does indeed last a lifetime, family is important, and if you need prayer, pray together.

Nanny keeps a prayer journal where she records all of her prayers for her family, friends, and even friends of friends for various needs, wants, or divine guidance. She also has pages upon pages of answers to those prayers.

In August of 2018, she joined my prayer that God send me a good man and for my time as a wife and mother to come. A month later, the man of my dreams appeared. He shares his son with me, and as future husband and wife, we hope to soon start making more children. So, there's another prayer Nanny can soon mark off as answered.

Pop, who's been my buddy since day one, always made sure we were treated better than gold. We helped him appraise cars at holiday mall sales, watched him get more excited about going to Disneyland than us, and went on countless trips to visit family or for quick vacations.

Our grandparents made sure our lives were full of Jesus, laughter, and unimaginable amounts of love. They have been so involved in all of our lives that we wouldn't be who we are without them.

—*Chezaraye Allnutt, Granddaughter*

However, since they weren't quite done, mom came to our home in Salinas for a few days in June of 2004. Together, we watched the funeral service for President Ronald Reagan in Washington, DC. We also tuned in that evening for his internment service at the Reagan Presidential Library in Simi Valley. When his son, Michael Reagan, gave his eulogy and talked about how his father treated everyone with unfailing courtesy, never making anyone feel small, and was such a great father, the memories of what family meant to me—and the profound loss of my father to the ravages of alcohol—touched a nerve deep within.

What really got to me, though, was a story Michael shared about the time he was on a flight from Washington, DC, to California with his father. It was late at night, and they were the only ones awake. President Reagan told his son how much Jesus Christ meant to him and how he had come to know Jesus as his Savior. His son then asked his father to pray for him so he too could make that decision.

My conversion had made such a dramatic impact on my life those twenty-five years of memories brought tears to my eyes. When mom asked what was bothering me, I explained the reason for my tears. That prompted her to ask a series of questions about salvation. After I answered them, she said she wanted Jesus to come into her heart too, which caused more tears. She started coming to church with us and even raised her arms whenever we did. It took more than twenty years of faithful prayers for her, but it was worth every minute because I know one day I will see mom again in heaven.

Signs of Trouble

We decided to sell our home in Salinas after Charlene and Frank sold their home nearby to move to England, where they planned to open a franchise of the popular Curves fitness center, which caters to a female clientele. At that time, I wanted to help my mother in San Jose since Billy had moved out, leaving her alone.

Wanting to see what God would do, we listed our home for double the price we had paid in 1996. It sold in a few days, and we moved into the open room in mom's two-bedroom home for a short time. Son Gavin had to bunk in the living room, sleeping on a fold-up bed.

After moving back to San Jose, I joined a twenty-four-hour fitness club. One day on my way back from a workout, I broke out into a sweat. My heart racing, I started shaking. Fortunately, I was just a few blocks from a longtime friend who had been our family doctor when we lived there before. After his nurse checked my vital signs, she told me I needed to go straight to the emergency room at Santa Clara Valley Medical Center, just two blocks away. She called a friend who worked there to let her know I was on the way.

When I talked to a nurse at the admitting desk, she called for an aide to bring a gurney and take me straight to the doctors to check me out. Although I told her I didn't feel that bad, she replied my blood pressure was more than 200 over 110 (normally mine read 120 over 80), and if the upper number hit 230, I could die on the table. I knew it was serious, especially when they started piling bags of ice onto my body. They finally brought my pressure down to 160 over 90. Since that was still too high, this incident launched a new era of taking blood pressure medication and seeking to reduce stress in my life.

In the meantime, we also set out on a search for a new, extended-family-size home where all of our aging relatives could stay with us. We finally settled on a spacious place in Oakdale, ninety miles from San Jose. It had plenty of space for both our mothers, who stayed in the two downstairs bedrooms. Soon after we moved in, my mother asked Esperanza Senior to sleep in the same room with her at night since her Alzheimer's was getting worse. She was so loving to my mother they became almost like sisters.

The move didn't slow down my search for a solution to my mysterious heart ailments. Among the questions I wanted answered is whether, under these conditions, it was all right for me to go to England to visit Charlene and her family. After consultations with several doctors, we felt it was safe. Some friends agreed to stay at our home to keep an eye on our mothers while we set off for a three-week adventure.

Merry Olde England

We landed at Gatwick Airport near Frank's hometown of Crawley. He picked us up and took us to a park next to the ocean in Brighton. This spectacular city had great views, fine restaurants, and friendly people. We arrived that day to sunny, clear skies and mild weather, making for a pleasant drive when Frank took us the last twenty miles to the family's home in Shoreham-by-Sea.

When we arrived, Charlene was at Curves with Cheza-raye, but Frankey and Zak were just coming home from school. We were excited to see them.

Later at dinner, we chatted about our trip, how the kids were adjusting to classes in England, and how Charlene was faring at Curves. She had previously owned one in Gonzales, a small town about fifteen miles south of Salinas. While business had started picking up lately, Charlene said it was still a struggle. I could relate. It seemed like most of my career had been a struggle, which is why I found such solace in my faith in God.

That vacation was special. While visiting England is a great vacation for anyone, having loved ones there to enjoy it with rates far higher on the life satisfaction scale. Seeing our loved ones again was a thrill, not to mention the relaxation of the longest vacation we had ever taken. I loved spending three weeks in my ancestral homeland. My sister-in-law's friend traced the Howell family bloodline all the way back to Leicestershire and Sir Thomas Payne, who was born in 1245.

During our stay, we visited Arundel, a historic town about thirty-miles southwest of Crawley and home to a medieval castle. A seventy-five-mile stretch of West Sussex contains ten castles; we literally could have spent three weeks just visiting them. There are some 1,500 castles in England, although many are only remnants of the historic fortresses that helped offer protection from the eleventh century on. Their beauty, splendor, and magnificence were a sight to behold.

While we stayed in Shoreham, Frank took us out to some great carvery restaurants, which is where cooked meat is freshly sliced to order, and old-time pubs with pool tables. The sad part of this story: Frank beat me in every game of pool or snooker we played, a humbling experience for a guy who in my teens cut my teeth on pool tables in San Jose and Santa Clara Valley.

Visit to London

Our vacation included a trip to London. We had to drive to Brighton to take the two-hour train ride into London. The train trip was exciting because of the sights we saw along the way, especially as we entered the bustling city. Once there, we stayed for four days at the Marriot Hotel, which is close to England's Parliament, London Bridge, and the London Eye—a Ferris wheel offering incredible views and the United Kingdom's most popular tourist attraction. That first night we took a short cab ride to the Hard Rock Café, which served the best hamburgers in town. The pictures of famous rock stars and guitars on the walls made us feel right at home.

The next day we ventured out to Buckingham Palace, hoping to see the Queen of England, but a palace guard said she was not coming in that day. Still, the grounds were splendid; they included the largest private garden in London. While the residence contains 775 rooms, most were roped off. Some of the walls had paintings of previous kings and queens—a total of seven thousand spread out across the royal palaces and residences. We looked at names like the Rubens, van Dyck, and Teniers from the seventeenth century, and Raphael, Bellini, Titian Correggio, Parmigianino, and Lorenz from the eighteenth.

Our next stop: the Tower of London, which also housed the royal jewels. We arrived just in time for the changing of the guard. The pomp and ceremony, including the perfection and timing of the whole event, was fantastic. Kings and queens have stored crowns, robes, and other items of their ceremonial regalia at the tower for some six centuries. Since the 1600s the coronation regalia, commonly known as the "Crown Jewels," have been protected at the tower.

That evening we went to the Royal Albert Hall to see the legendary *The Phantom of the Opera*, with music by Andrew Lloyd Webber. The music and acting were magnificent, although I found the mystery a bit confusing. In the end, I asked Espe about the deeper meaning. She prayed and asked the Lord what was happening and why, and to help us understand. God told her that the woman was madly in love with the phantom, but the phantom could not take her with him to hell because perfect love not only casts out fear, but the devil and hell cannot accept perfect love. That message still sends shivers up my spine.

More Sightseeing

While in London, we decided to do our shopping on Oxford Street, home to more than three hundred shops, designer stores, and various landmarks. After stopping at several, Espe ended up with two pairs of shoes, and I bought a heavy coat. We had a great lunch; I told Londoners we chatted with that the area reminded me of downtown San Francisco's shopping area. That day we also visited the SoHo area in the town of Westminster, as well as Piccadilly Circus and Carnaby Street. The latter is near Abbey Road, which the Beatles made famous. As we grabbed the train back to Brighton, we talked about what a great trip it had been and how we would love to return to see more of London's beauty and history.

We had only a few days to rest up for the next side trip Espe and Charlene had scheduled to the Mediterranean islands of Majorca, Spain. We all flew there to visit Espe's Aunt Tania, who lived in a six-bedroom villa owned by her son-in-law. Majorca has five islands with just over nine hundred thousand people living on them; we stayed on the largest island of Palma.

With an average year-round temperature of seventy-one degrees, Majorca reminded me of the Hawaiian Islands. Its history goes back to prehistoric settlements, making it quite popular with tourists from Germany and the United Kingdom. After our go-go visit to London, we had a great time just relaxing and visiting with extended family. Each daughter in the group had a small child, and everyone had a ball playing with them, especially in the swimming pool. We also took a tour around the island; we loved downtown by the beach, where multimillion-dollar yachts were docked.

Given the physical problems that had been bothering me, our visit to England was the perfect stress reliever. After returning to Oakdale, we settled into a more relaxed lifestyle.

However, as much as we enjoyed our two years there, bigger changes were in store. I knew my high blood pressure could spell serious problems, yet the family doctor and specialists I visited in nearby Modesto could not find anything wrong with my heart. I would only find the help I needed after our final, major move—to Las Vegas.

CHAPTER 14

Quest for Healing

"Hear me when I call, O God of my righteousness!
You have relieved me in my distress. Have mercy
on me and hear my prayer."

Psalm 4:1

By now, you have likely formed the idea that I like to move and can make impulsive decisions. That's the best way to explain how, just two years after relocating to our extended family-sized home in Oakdale, California, we pulled up stakes and headed for Las Vegas. As is so often the case, family had a lot to do with it.

Despite her disastrous experience in Los Gatos, Espe had been wanting to try her hand at another Mexican restaurant.

Despite my misgivings, Espe persuaded me to finance a new restaurant in Las Vegas. We moved there in November of 2007 and opened Espe's Gourmet Tamales the following spring. Ironically, although I hadn't been too keen about moving there, that's where I found the answer to my mysterious heart problems. That had concerned me ever since that day in 2003 when I sensed the Lord telling me I would die if I stayed much longer at Sam Linder Honda in Salinas.

Yet, no one seemed able to help. I visited doctors in Salinas, San Jose, and Modesto, but everyone insisted I was fine. I finally found the right heart specialist by flipping through the Yellow Pages (remember them?) of the Las Vegas telephone directory: Dr. Zia Kahn. I started seeing him soon after the opening of Espe's Gourmet Tamales. Dr. Kahn ran a series of tests in hopes of pinpointing the source of my problems.

I'm fortunate that I didn't have a major incident any sooner than I did after the blowup that followed the restaurant opening. As you may remember, 2008 brought on the Great Recession. Meanwhile, although everyone raved about Espe's food, no matter how hard we worked, the losses mounted, and we closed in June of 2009.

Chezaraye, promotion staff member, and Frankey

"Hanging Tamale Memories"

Anyone can stand up and say that something is special and valuable, but none of it matters that much unless it's special to you. Our family created Espe's Gourmet Tamales, and together we made it special. I treasure all the memories from that experience for multiple reasons:

- The idea blossomed within Grandma's heart.

- My aunt and uncle gave it their all to ensure a business could feel like a home.
- My cousins and I could eat the food and feel the warmth and love built into the recipe itself.
- It was also special, not because we were proud of what we created, but because we did it together.

In a world of unpredictability, instability, and problems brought on by the Great Recession, not even hard work, dedication, and prayer could save a family business. But in the same way, a parent hangs their child's artwork on the refrigerator; we hung the memory of Espe's Gourmet Tamales forever in our hearts.

The world would call the restaurant a failure, but not our family. In life, profit-and-loss statements aren't all that matters.

—*Elizabeth Anderson, Granddaughter*

However, right before we closed, my stress reached a boiling point. While granddaughter Frankey and I were passing out restaurant flyers at a shopping center, I had to stop after suddenly struggling to breathe. Fran-

QUEST FOR HEALING

key reached for her cell phone and called her mother, Charlene. She met us at our restaurant and drove us to Summerlin Hospital, where Dr. Kahn was performing a heart procedure. When he finally tried to admit me to one of his heart surgery centers, they were finished for the day. He told me all his tests had shown a healthy heart, but this episode would require an angiogram at the hospital. He scheduled one for 7:00 a.m. the next day.

I tossed and turned all night. Finally, the time came. After preparations and instructions for the procedure, Dr. Kahn told me this was his last test, and he hoped everything would prove positive. I remained alert during the angiogram, which started at 8:30 a.m. Dr. Kahn and two doctors assisting him made a small incision on my right side for the camera that would take different views. All I could see that well was Dr. Kahn's face. It alarmed me when he seemed shocked, and sweat trickled down his face.

"Uh, I need to take out the blockage to your main artery," he said. The last thing I heard before passing out: "It's over 90 percent blocked."

About two hours later, I woke up. Dr. Kahn had told Espe that if he had not removed the blockage, I would have died in less than a week. It took six years of searching, but I had finally found the doctor who went the extra mile. He proved it not only then but a few years later when he started testing blood flow in my legs by putting gel on them and doing an ultrasound. He did the same procedure annually; after the fourth test, he said, "you have a blockage."

He scheduled me for a procedure at a surgery center in Las Vegas, which identified a 90 percent blockage in the main vein of my left leg and a 70 percent blockage elsewhere in the right leg. With two more stents added, I feel fine and appreciate everything Dr. Kahn does to keep me alive and healthy. This kind of care is why I plan to live out the rest of my days in Las Vegas.

Touring Las Vegas

When many people think of Las Vegas, the first thing that comes to mind is the famed Strip and the casinos, live entertainment, and gambling that go on 24/7. But most residents rarely visit there, and then usually to take in a particular show or give family or friends from out of town the so-called ten-dollar tour.

When visitors come, I offer my services as the area's best free tour guide. I start with the new shopping center suburban Summerlin's downtown before stopping at nearby Las Vegas Ballpark. It's home to baseball's Aviators, a class AAA affiliate of the Oakland Athletics. After stopping at the National Hockey League expansion franchise's Golden Knights' practice facility, I drive about seven miles west to the Red Rock Canyon

National Conservation Area's visitors center. Then we go on the 12.5-mile loop around the canyon, including several scenic stops. The views include watching climbers scaling the mountain wall and a gorgeous backdrop of the Las Vegas skyline.

Afterward, we can stop for lunch at the Red Rock Casino buffet or an array of choice restaurants in a nearby mall. Next comes the Hoover Dam, one of eight construction miracles in the Great Depression of the 1930s. It supplies water for Las Vegas, Los Angeles, and Arizona. When we come back to town, we park at the Bellagio Hotel parking structure so we can see the latest display in their conservatory—a new one is erected during each of the four seasons. In front of the hotel stands the Fountains of Bellagio, which offer daily water shows, each set to different forms of music. Tram rides are available to other sights and hotels as well as a new arena for the Las Vegas Knights hockey team and special events.

We can also go across the street to a rather new attraction: the High Roller Observation Wheel, one of the largest in the world. They have created a great walkway between the LINQ and Flamingo hotels, with restaurants and entertainment, including a bowling alley with thirty-two lanes.

To end the day, we head downtown to Fremont Street Experience and stop at the famous Gold & Silver

Pawn Shop or our new auditorium, the Smith Center for the Performing Arts. Of course, since the NFL came to Las Vegas in 2020, many sightseers also want to take a side trip to see the Raiders' new Allegiant Stadium.

The one thing that doesn't automatically come to mind when people think of Las Vegas is church. And if it does, it's often linked to one of the twenty-four-hour wedding chapels that dot the city.

However, Las Vegas has great churches and pastors. For six years, we were blessed to attend Cornerstone Christian Fellowship, where Senior Pastor Greg Massanari marked his thirtieth anniversary in 2015, our final year there. I understand that Pastor Greg stepped down a few years later to become the head of their Christian school and turned over his pastoral duties to his son, Joey. Christmas and Easter services at Cornerstone were always special, and many of Pastor Greg's sermons touched our hearts. He also ministered to me when we had to close Espe's restaurant, and I suffered from depression.

Since 2015 we have attended Canyon Ridge Christian Church in the north part of Las Vegas. Our daughter, Charlene, helps take up Sunday offerings and serves as an usher during Communion. It is a large church, with a Saturday afternoon and two Sunday services. We go to the 11:00 a.m. service on Sundays; a good friend, Norman, always saves us seats in the front row. We have made great friendships there, and the staff is friendly and helpful in many ways. The pastors that preach from the Bible are knowledgeable, sincere, and truthful about Jesus Christ and His life that provides our salvation.

A New Venture

Despite the physical challenges that I mentioned earlier, in the midst of them in 2012, I was feeling quite healthy and ready for anything that came my way. Just then, an old friend called me to discuss working for his business as a regional representative for a company based on the East Coast, Live Event Stream Automotive. It offered high-tech video displays to car dealers.

Using Live Event Stream, customers could see a video of a dealer's inventory on their smartphones or the dealership's website (by March of 2020, they had approximately seven hundred dealers across the nation using their product). It involved using a camera to film a dealership's new and used vehicles, with a walkaround of each unit of five to seven minutes. This allowed for a complete view of the outside, interior, and trunk space. The dealer could use the company's software to download all the videos and put them on the dealer's website.

The timing for California was perfect. My friend had signed up some dealers in Southern California and wanted to expand beyond that region. After reviewing the information he sent me and researching their product, I felt good about it. So, I traveled to Southern California to see one of their initial installations and meet the owner, Phillip, and his partner, Tom. After we all had dinner together, they assigned me Northern California.

Thanks to all my past contacts there, within two weeks, I had lined up half a dozen appointments. My friend, Bill Owen and Tom came to San Jose for our first appointment on a Monday morning with a Ford dealer in suburban Morgan Hill. Soon after we arrived, the dealer came out, told Tom he was already convinced to buy our product, and to "explain everything to my general manager and sales managers."

Looking at me and smiling, Tom said: "That was my easiest close ever."

Our next stop was about an hour north of Morgan Hill. After meeting with the Chevrolet dealership's general manager, Tom racked another "yes" in the sales column. We all left happy and excited about the next day.

On Tuesday, our first meeting was with a Lexus dealer in Fremont. He too felt this program was perfect and signed up after Tom's presentation. After lunch, we went to the Toyota dealer in Sunnyvale, the Bay Area's leader in sales. Although Tom masterfully answered numerous questions, we didn't convince him to sign until two weeks later. Our next meeting on Wednesday was with another Toyota dealer in Redwood City; Jim Rimmer was an old friend from my Don Lucas days in San Jose. Tom closed another deal and returned to Texas, excited about our success.

Once we signed up dealers, I used son Gavin to train their photo crews on the process. The fastest way initially to get them online was for Gavin, Espe, and I to film all the vehicles. Depending on the size of the dealership, we could complete that task in two to six days. Our largest dealership was Sunnyvale Toyota, which had an inventory of 750 new and 200 used vehicles.

In addition to Northern California, we signed up more dealers in Las Vegas, such as Gaudin Jaguar, Land Rover of Las Vegas, and Reliable Auto Sales. I ended up with fifteen dealerships in Northern California and Las Vegas. I had to oversee the region after the friend who persuaded me to get involved got in a dispute with the company and dissolved ties. While I worked directly for the company for a couple of years, the business started to trail off about the same time I fell while visiting my granddaughter's gym in October of 2015. A chair collapsed, and I injured my head, neck, and back, meaning I have to now use a cane most of the time.

A Day to Remember

One event we will cherish for the rest of our lives is our fiftieth wedding anniversary on July 23, 2016.

People came from near and far away: California, Texas, Colorado, Illinois, New Mexico, New York, and Mexico to help us celebrate. About forty-five people jammed into the small Cupid's Wedding Chapel in Las Vegas to watch us renew our vows. When we got married in 1966, the wedding director and a stranger were the only witnesses.

Our first time in Cupid's Chapel, we were two wet-behind-the-ears young adults. This time we walked in with flair and style. I wore full cowboy attire, including hat and boots—accompanied by a host of supporters. Our grandson Zakerey played the guitar while Espe's brother, Eddie, played the conga drums. They provided the music for a Johnny Cash impersonator, who performed some of the legendary country singer's popular tunes.

Finally, my beautiful bride came down the aisle, wearing a sparkling white outfit and a smile to match. Our great-grandchildren, Peyton, Jacob, and Mariah, tossed flower petals as they led Espe to the altar amid the sounds of "I Walk the Line." Finally, the Johnny Cash impersonator led us in our vows, taking longer than normal because he sang four more songs during the ceremony.

Naturally, everyone snapped lots of photos, and we hired a professional videographer to record the day's events. They concluded with a backyard wedding reception and swimming party at our home. Our seventy-plus guests included family, relatives, and longtime friends. We appreciate everyone who traveled such long distances, or just across town, to be with us on that most memorable day.

"The Epitome of Bliss"

Imagine this: You are publicly declaring your continuing love for your spouse of fifty years. You enter the same chapel where you were married to see the place filled to capacity with your brothers and sisters, nieces and nephews, children, and grandchildren. Your great-grandchildren, decked in cowboy boots, walk down the aisle as your ring bearer and flower girls. You are surrounded by your progeny—your legacy.

You think to yourself that this moment couldn't get any better. Then, you look toward the front of the chapel and see that Johnny Cash is standing next to the love of your life, eager to officiate your fiftieth-anniversary vows.

This was the scene in 2016 as I watched my grandparents renew their vows. Their love for each other was clearly written on their faces as they held hands and stared deeply into each other's eyes. It was almost surreal—a moment straight out of a Hallmark movie.

The cinematic elements of the ceremony were furthered by the Johnny Cash imitator leading us in a song as my cousin Zak happily strummed his guitar. Laughter, singing, clapping, and dancing filled the chapel with joy! We immersed ourselves in their love as if it were palpable. It was truly a sight to behold. I will remember this day forever as the epitome of marital bliss.

—*Sarah Williams, Granddaughter*

Serving God

When I came to know Jesus as my Lord and Savior in 1979, I was so grateful I wanted to serve Him in any way I could. That's why, as mentioned in chapter six, we opened our home in Hillsborough and Las Gatos for worship, Bible study, and prayer meetings. Everything we have done and are still doing today is for God's glory. We follow His leading, especially when we are called to homes or hospitals to pray about sickness or illnesses or for end-of-life prayer and ministry.

There are many examples of the latter: starting with one of Espe's uncles, Santiago "Sam" Troncoso. While we were staying with Espe's uncle Jose Troncoso in Monrovia, California, while hiring staffers for a new call center, we learned from another one of Espe's uncles that Sam, the Hollywood actor, which Espe's family had lived with for a few months in 1956, was in Monrovia Hospital. So, that evening, we went to see Uncle Sam. We didn't know he had only three more days to live. He was in good spirits, joking with us and recalling the good old days.

When we went back to see Sam the next afternoon, his good humor had faded. His liver was failing, leaving his body quite weak. Espe said to her uncle: "Do you want to accept Jesus Christ in your heart and go to heaven? Open your eyes two times." He blinked twice, and I held his hand and led him in a prayer to accept

Jesus as Lord. When we returned later that evening, he passed away; shortly after midnight he went to heaven on May 29, 1993.

Several years later, we went to visit Espe's father, Alberto. He was in a rest home in Salinas. Espe and her brother, Eddie, went to the rest home. As they were walking down the hall to their father's room, Eddie asked: "Has our father accepted the Lord?"

"To my knowledge, no," she replied.

Once they entered, Eddie expressed his desire to pray with his father. Alberto agreed, and Eddie led him a prayer of salvation, which brought this sign of acceptance from his father: "Sí." On January 18, 2000, Alberto passed into the arms of the Lord. What a difference that decision made a few days later at his funeral. We were able to share with numerous family members from Southern California, Texas, and Mexico about the eternal decision Alberto had made just days earlier.

The following year, Espe and I received a call about Nick Mendez, an old friend from 4th Street Bowl days in San Jose. Like Billy, after school, Nick had gone to barber school and even worked for three years at Billy's barbershop. Whenever I went to Billy's shop for a haircut, Nick and I always had great times talking about family, new events in our lives, and recalling the good old days.

With his characteristic sense of humor, Billy had labeled Nick "Big Time." That came from Nick playing on the San Jose High football team in 1958 with offensive guard and future pro star Jim Cadile. Drafted out of San Jose State College in 1962 by the Chicago Bears, Cadile made All-Pro eight times in eleven seasons and was later elected to the Pro Football Hall of Fame in Canton, Ohio.

Now, Nick was in Santa Clara Kaiser Hospital for what appeared his final days. Although quite sick, he was awake when we arrived. We were able to minister the love of Christ to him and discuss Scripture verses. After we did, we asked if he wanted to accept Jesus into his heart.

"Yes," he replied.

We led him to Christ not long before he passed away on August 15, 2001. Espe and I will always remember Nick as a loving husband to his wife, Carmen, and father to his children as well as the protector of his father, mother, and younger brother.

Old Memories

All those childhood memories from San Jose surfaced again when my mother, Alyce Irene Gilliam, died on February 15, 2007. We had the service at Oak Hill Funeral Home in San Jose a few days later. Our old friend Father Bush honored our family by doing the last rites and service. At a special luncheon afterward, I was able to share how my mother came to know Jesus Christ as her Lord and Savior while watching President Regan's internment service. I told the audience that I knew she was now in heaven because of her faith in her Savior.

Espe's mother, Esperanza Senior, would follow my mom to the grave on February 16, 2014. She had a Catholic service at Saint Lawrence the Martyr in Santa Clara, with five priests and a bishop at the altar to perform a requiem mass and Communion. Our brother-in-law, Richard Haro, put everything together and participated in the service.

The good news is after years of fighting against the idea of being born again, Esperanza Senior had given her heart to Christ in June of 2011. Once she had, she bought a Spanish-language large print Bible. Every day for three hours, she and Espe studied the Word of God, which brought them closer to Him. It produced wisdom, knowledge, and a better understanding of His purpose for their lives. As they read and prayed together, they sensed God's unbelievable love for them. Espe will never forget those precious moments.

One reason Esperanza Senior was so special to us is she and her husband, Alberto, lived with us for most of our married life. The primary reason Espe stayed with me during my thirteen years of selfishness, craziness, and stupidity before I decided to follow Jesus came from her parents urging her to stay with me for the sake of our children and marriage. Looking back on those years, I must thank God, Esperanza Senior, and Alberto for keeping Espe and I together.

Just as Espe's mother made the decision that changed her life, three years later, so would my brother, Billy. In August of 2017, his son, Willie, called me to tell me his father was fading fast. Espe and I drove to the Eisenhower Medical Center in Rancho Mirage, California, just south of Palm Springs. When we finally found his room, we noticed he was a bit disoriented and expressing concern over his condition. When we talked with the nurses to see what in the heck was going on, they said they were still waiting for the results of his medical tests.

When we returned the next day, nothing had been resolved. So, I asked Billy if he wanted us to pray for him. He nodded. Afterward, I asked my brother if he wanted to accept Jesus Christ into his heart. After he nodded again, we led him in a salvation prayer. That weekend when old friends Hector and Lydia came from San Jose to see him, Billy was like himself again, telling jokes and laughing. A week later, Willie called and said the tests were bad, and there was no way to operate; he had given the doctors my phone number. Soon, one called and asked me about Billy's lifestyle. When I told him the truth about Billy's wild past, the physician replied: "That explains everything."

On September 2, 2017, my brother passed away. Three weeks later, Willie organized a ceremony of life at Christ of the Desert Church in Palm Desert. I was so thankful to be able to share the story of how Billy was now in heaven because of the decision he had made to accept Christ just days earlier.

"Ideate"

Uncle Buzz is my dad's older brother.

He's also married to my mom's older sister. As a result, we were a tight-knit extended family. I share the same sets of grandparents as Uncle Buzz's children. When I was a kid, my dad liked taking me to Bay Area sporting events, where we saw the Oakland A's, Oakland Raiders, San Francisco Giants, San Francisco 49ers, Golden State Warriors, San Jose Sharks, and the San Jose Earthquakes. Often, Uncle Buzz would attend the sporting events, too, with his kids. So, we would all go as one big extended family.

My dad also took me bowling often. He learned to bowl at San Jose's 4th Street Bowl along with Uncle Buzz when they were teenagers. And we would often go golfing together. I ended up playing varsity golf for my high school and winning a state title my senior year.

My dad's mother, Grandma Alyce, used to take her sons, my dad and Uncle Buzz to the live boxing matches at the San Jose Civic Auditorium. One of their favorite fighters to watch perform back then in the late '50s/early '60s was Luis Molina, a staple at the Civic Auditorium fights. Grandma Alyce used to also host Saturday evening family nights at her house, where our extended family would gather to watch championship fights broadcast on cable TV's HBO and Showtime in the 1990s and 2000s. My dad and Uncle Buzz's childhood friend Hector "Hec-n-Bro" Rodriguez would also attend those family nights. Uncle Buzz got serious about his faith while I was still a tween.

I remember he would have Bible studies and prayer groups at his house. He would also regularly attend church services and do volunteer ministry. My dad did not share the same passion for his faith as Uncle Buzz. However, they had mutual respect and always cared for and loved each other. That was evident.

I would say my fondest memories with my extended family, including Uncle Buzz, were the times we went water and snow skiing. There was a time when Uncle Buzz had a boat and a summer/winter vacation home near a popular Northern California recreational lake and ski resort. Those were joyous times. I am happy Uncle Buzz wrote this book, and I hope you enjoy the stories and the message within its pages.

—*William Howell, nephew*

William Howell with Brandon, Malia Star, and Kristian

More Soul-Winning

The next year in May, Espe and I were vacationing at our time-share at Newport Beach, California when Espe called her Uncle Enrique in Azusa to say hello. He told Espe he was at the hospital with his son, Ricky, who has been in a coma for two days. I had known Ricky since he was seven years old and served as the ring bearer at our wedding.

After Ricky grew up, he married a woman named Martha. We reconnected when they bought a home in Hollister, about forty-five miles south of Las Gatos. Ricky and Martha came to our prayer meetings in Los Gatos, where both accepted Christ. We later went to visit them several times at their home. Those visits ended after we went to see them and discovered they had bought a rabbit for their son, little Ricky; that day, I discovered I was allergic to rabbit fur. After their marriage ended, Ricky went to stay with his father in Azusa. Martha moved to Seattle, Washington, and is still in contact with Espe.

When we arrived at the hospital in Glendora, Ricky proved unresponsive. A few minutes later, Espe and I prayed over him in the name of Jesus, asking that he wake up and rededicate his life to Jesus. Nothing. His father said he had been that way for the last two days. His room was twenty feet from the nurses' station, and suddenly they were yelling, "Dr. Basilio is here!"

The doctor was also named Basil; I told him he was the only Basil I had ever met in person before giving him a big hug. We talked for a while when suddenly I looked behind me to see a nurse walking down the hall with Ricky. When Espe and I got to his room, Ricky was wearing his famous smile, proclaiming his joy about his salvation. He died two days later, on May 30, 2019.

On November 2 of 2019, I received a call from my old friend Marshall Mendez about our mutual friend Hector Rodriguez. Hector was in serious condition at El Camino Hospital in Mountain View, California, with a cancerous tumor in his stomach. Marshall wasn't doing too well either. He was at the Veterans Administration hospital in Palo Alto after an operation that cost him two toes and part of his foot.

We left hurriedly at 7:00 a.m. on Sunday, November 3, and made good time in the fairly new rental car until we were about a hundred miles from Bakersfield, California. When strange noises started coming from the engine, we pulled off an exit ramp and into a gas station. There I called the rental car company. They wanted the car towed to Fresno. Once we made it to the Fresno airport, they gave us another car. That set us back a few hours, but we still made it to our hotel room in Sunnyvale by 3:30 p.m. After checking in, we changed and drove to the hospital.

There were many family members present: Hector's wife, Lydia; son Hector and his wife and their two sons, son Vincent and his wife with their son and daughter, and numerous assorted relatives and friends. Espe and I have been in many hospitals, but I don't ever remember seeing someone so happy and joyous in a hospital bed like Hector. We were there for nearly five hours, and Hector smiled as many people came into the room. Unable to speak too loudly, he would whisper and ask me to share old stories about the 4th Street Bowl; his smiles were something I will treasure for the rest of my life.

After everyone left around nine o'clock, Espe, Lydia, and I prayed for Hector to make it through this illness. I also prayed with Hector, asking if he wanted to accept Jesus Christ as his Savior. Bending low to hear his soft voice, I heard him yell out "yes!" with a big smile on his face. We left rejoicing and returned to see him for two more days.

A Final Trip

That Monday, we were able to visit with Marshall and his wife, Evelyn, for several hours at the VA hospital. We also went by their home later to see Evelyn and get reacquainted with their oldest son, Nick, whom we hadn't seen in years.

The next day we returned for visits at both hospitals. While we heard a good report in Marshall's room, it wasn't so at Hector's. The tumor in his stomach had spread to his back, yet his spirit was strong, and his faith was powerful. Three months after we first visited Hector, we learned that he was feeling great, had gained eighteen pounds, and had returned home. Still, on April 6, 2020, we received the horrible news that he had lost his final battle with cancer. The thought that comforts me is knowing he went straight to heaven and will be there for my second visit.

> For the kingdom of heaven is like a landowner who went out early in the morning to hire laborers for his vineyard. Now when he had agreed with the laborers for a denarius a day, he sent them into his vineyard. And he went out about the third hour and saw others standing idle in the marketplace, and said to them, 'You also go into the vineyard, and whatever is right I will give you.' So they went. Again he went out about the sixth and the ninth hour, and did likewise. And about the eleventh hour he went out and found others standing idle, and said to them, 'Why have you been standing here idle all day?' They said to him, 'Because no one hired us.' He said

to them, 'You also go into the vineyard, and whatever is right you will receive.'

So when evening had come, the owner of the vineyard said to his steward, 'Call the laborers and give them their wages, beginning with the last to the first.' And when those came who were hired about the eleventh hour, they each received a denarius. But when the first came, they supposed that they would receive more; and they likewise received each a denarius. And when they had received it, they complained against the landowner, saying, 'These last men have worked only one hour, and you made them equal to us who have borne the burden and the heat of the day.' But he answered one of them and said, 'Friend, I am doing you no wrong. Did you not agree with me for a denarius? Take what is yours and go your way. I wish to give to this last man the same as to you. Is it not lawful for me to do what I wish with my own things? Or is your eye evil because I am good?' So the last will be first, and the first last. For many are called, but few chosen.

Matthew 20:1-16

What this passage means to me is even though I accepted Jesus as my Savior forty years before Hector did, my reward will be the same as anyone who accepts Christ in the last hour of their life. The Christian friends and family reunion will be spectacular!

Before going home to Las Vegas after our emergency trip, we took one last drive down Memory Lane. We started at Santa Clara University, where Albert had earned his bachelor's degree. Then it was on to San Jose, where we were amazed at how much the downtown area had changed. There were more tall buildings and congestion and streetcars up and down First and Second Street. My old homestead at 237 North 4th Street was still a vacant lot, while the St. Patrick's Catholic Church on 9th Street was gone too, burned to the ground. My old elementary school, Horace Mann, had been rebuilt and looked like a fortress. While 4th Street Bowl looked the same, most of the pool tables had been replaced by a counter offering bowling supplies for sale.

Next, we drove out to Stevens Creek Boulevard and passed by the Santana Row shopping area that used to be home to Courtesy Chevrolet, with the Valley Fair (now Westfield Valley Fair) shopping mall undergoing another remodeling. Then we came to "auto row"—Stevens Creek Boulevard, where I had started as a salesman at the now-defunct Bob Sykes Dodge in 1964, and later worked as a sales manager at Auto Car Europe-Volvo/Fiat.

"Snow-Covered Memories"

About four months after Buzz's trip down Memory Lane, my wife, Wilma, and I returned to San Jose. We went to see Velma Hoffer, who, along with her husband, Walt, were leaders at Crossroads during Buzz and Espe's time there. After Walt's death in 2015, Wilma (and sometimes me) regularly flew back to see Velma. This time, I even made an appointment to see Crossroads' current pastor, but he canceled because of sickness.

I don't know if that was related to coronavirus, but the pandemic directly affected us. We had planned to fly back to Denver in mid-March of 2020, but because of the virus, we knew we needed to stay a couple of days longer. Her daughter, who lived close by and usually saw that Velma had food and supplies, couldn't get out of the house because of virus fears. In addition, our children urged us to avoid airports.

Then came the city's order to shelter in place. We had until midnight that Monday to leave. Canceling our flight, we rented a car and headed north on I-80. Any Californian knows to avoid that route because of Donner Pass, a mountain range commonly socked in by snow. I should have known too, but I guess under pressure, my brain short-circuited.

When we saw big rigs parked on the shoulder, I realized laws mandating tire chains were in effect. We turned around and headed south, finding a motel room for a brief rest. At dawn, we headed to Bakersfield and then east to Barstow to pick up I-40. Once again, the prospect of snow or ice loomed at Flagstaff, Arizona. Fortunately, we got fifty miles beyond danger before stopping for the night.

As memorable as that trip was, I mostly recall the wonderful years of ministry we enjoyed in the Santa Clara Valley. As pastors, we wanted to impact others for the Lord. But the fact is: they greatly affected our lives. Thanks, Buzz and Espe, for the remainder of those years! We now enjoy a deeper walk in the power of the Holy Spirit. That is something that will last forever.

—*Rich Marshall*
Buzz Howell's former pastor

To echo George Bailey in the familiar Christmas movie, despite the pain and challenges along the way, it really has been a wonderful life. And yet, an even better one is coming—the day I step into heaven—again.

I invite you to accept Jesus Christ as your Lord and Savior.

"Jesus answered and said to him, 'Most assuredly, I say to you, unless one is born again, he cannot see the kingdom of God.'"

John 3:3

"For God so loved the world that He gave His only begotten Son, that whoever believes in Him should not perish but have everlasting life."

John 3:16

A simple prayer asking Jesus Christ to come into your heart with sincere repentance (the key to God's heart also releases His love) means He will forgive your past sins.

Endnotes

Chapter 1
Verification of Heaven
1 Don Piper with Cecil Murphey, *90 Minutes in Heaven: A True Story of Death and Life* (Grand Rapids, MI: Revell, 2014, 10th Anniversary Edition), 25.
2 Ibid.

CPSIA information can be obtained
at www.ICGtesting.com
Printed in the USA
LVHW052114200921
698283LV00012B/344